Department of Defense Biological Safety and Security Program

May 2009

Office of the Under Secretary of Defense
For Acquisition, Technology, and Logistics
Washington,   D.C.   20301-3140

**DEFENSE SCIENCE
BOARD**

MEMORANDUM FOR UNDER SECRETARY OF DEFENSE FOR
ACQUISITION, TECHNOLOGY AND LOGISTICS

SUBJECT: Final Report of the Defense Science Board Task Force on Department
of Defense Biological Safety and Security Program

I am pleased to forward the final report of the Defense Science Board Task
Force on the Department of Defense (DoD) Biological Safety and Security
Program.

This report examines the biological safety, security, and personnel reliability
programs of DoD's biological labs, compares these labs with other similar
operations in academia, industry and the federal government. The report offers
recommendations for improvements in the DoD program based on this
comparison.

The task force found that safety and security of the DoD facilities that they
assessed are as good or better than those in comparably sized facilities in other
government, industry and academic sectors and that DoD regulations exceed those
imposed by the Centers for Disease Control and Prevention. While the program
remains sound, the task force does provide recommendations to further improve
on computer systems security, lab activity monitoring, inspection compliance and
biological select agent and toxin transportation. These recommendations are
detailed in the report and serve to further enhance current biological safety and
security operations, while minimizing the impact on missions of the DoD
laboratories.

I endorse all of the study's recommendations and encourage you to forward
the report to the Secretary of Defense.

William Schneider, Jr.
DSB Chairman

MEMORANDUM FOR: Chairman, Defense Science Board

SUBJECT: Final Report of the Defense Science Board Task Force on
the Department of Defense Biological Safety and Security Program

Maintaining the safety of Department of Defense (DoD) personnel working on and around biological select agents and toxins (BSATs), coupled with maintaining the security of BSAT, is vital to the mission of DoD. To that end, the task force tried to answer the following questions: Are current and proposed policies to protect, use, store and transport BSATs sufficiently stringent? Are personnel reliability programs adequate to protect against insider threats, to the degree possible and commensurate with the threat? Do operations in the Department compare favorably with those in other government, academic, and industry laboratories? These questions are among those posed to the task force as it examined the status of the DoD program.

Based on a series of briefings and site visits, and the experience of task force members, the single overarching finding of this investigation is that **a determined adversary cannot be prevented from obtaining very dangerous biological materials intended for nefarious purposes, if not from DoD laboratories, then from other sources. The nation needs to recognize this reality and be prepared to mitigate the effects of a biological attack. Today, we as a nation are not prepared.**

The task force addressed the DoD biological safety and security program from an end-to-end perspective in order to assess the proper balance of policies, regulations, and challenges in conducting research involving biological select agents and toxins. It found that DoD facilities are as good or better than those in comparably sized facilities in other government, industry, and academic sectors. The task force identified seven important areas where improvements could be made:

- **Cyber red team**. Use red teams to determine the presumed "isolation" of computer systems for preventing access through external connections. A different team, familiar with lab functionality should determine the ways a malefactor might subvert the systems. Mitigation plans, based on the results of such assessments, need to be developed and implemented.

- **Monitoring activities.** Make changes to monitoring activities to improve effectiveness without introducing overly intrusive measures. Hold periodic meetings with laboratory personnel to reinforce values, moral obligations, and observations that should be reported

- **Biological Personnel Reliability Program.** Maintain the use of this program, tailored to bio-defense work. As with other policies, balance risk of a malevolent insider against detriment to the laboratory mission.

- **Overseas regulations.** Use Department of State background investigations for host country personnel working in BSAT labs outside the United States. Issue waiver authority so that laboratory commanders can determine appropriate security measures for shipments into these facilities.

- **Compliance inspections.** Provide resources for a single, independent inspection team, comprised of authoritative individuals, for all DoD laboratories.

- **BSAT transport.** Review the usefulness of the two-person rule in preventing insider threats. Use "lost in the crowd" approach for shipments into laboratories. And consider the potential use of flight safe, tamper-resistant shipping containers.

- **Public education and relations.** An important element of biological safety and security is public education. Communication and public relations plans should be developed that include information on facility mission, safety measures, and emergency response plans.

Collectively, these recommendations will enhance current biological safety and security operations at DoD laboratories while minimizing the impact of regulatory processes on their missions. The costs of implementing these recommendations is believed to be modest, but should not be imposed on the research programs that affect the missions of the labs.

Mr. Larry Lynn
Chairman

North and South America

Winnipeg, Canada
Frederick, Maryland
Richmond, Virginia
Atlanta, Georgia
Galveston, Texas
San Antonio, Texas
Sao Paulo, Brazil

Europe

Minsk, Belarus
Colindale, England
London, England
Porton Down, England
Potters Bar, England
Lyon, France
Marburg, Germany
Hamburg, Germany
Milan, Italy
Rome, Italy
Valdeolmos, Spain
Mittelausen, Switzerland
Solna, Sweden
Ceské Budějovice, Czech Republic

Africa

Grahamstown, South Africa
Franceville, Gabon

Asia and Australia

Moscow, Russia
Novosibirsk, Siberia
Hyderabad, India
Bhopal, India
Taiwan, China
Tokyo, Japan
Geelong, Australia
Melbourne, Australia
Coopers Plains, Australia
Singapore

Biosafety level 4 facilities worldwide

Table of Contents

Executive Summary

The anthrax events of 2001, coupled with a continued threat of biological terrorism, create a significant imperative to develop defensive capabilities that protect against biological weapons. During the last few years, the Department of Health and Human Services and the Department of Homeland Security initiated efforts to increase the infrastructure, public health response, and research to develop medical remedies against identified biological select agents and toxins (BSATs). For decades, the Department of Defense (DoD) has maintained limited capability to develop defensive medical countermeasures against BSATs. In conjunction with these activities, DoD established minimum safety and security standards for safeguarding BSATs against theft, loss, diversion, or unauthorized access or use, and to conduct research in a safe, secure, and reliable manner.

Concerned about the current safety and security of BSATs, the Under Secretary of Defense for Acquisition, Technology, and Logistics (USD (AT&L)), with support of the secretaries of the three military departments, asked the chairman of the Defense Science Board to charter a task force to take a fresh look at the status of the biological safety, security, and personnel reliability programs of the Army, Navy and Air Force labs; compare these labs with other similar operations in academia, industry, and the federal government; and make recommendations for improvements in the DoD program. The terms of reference charged the task force to address the following specific issues:

- adequacy of current and proposed policies
- use, storage, and transport of BSATs meeting stringent standards for safety, security, and personnel reliability
- comparison of operations in DoD with similar operations in other government, academic, and industry labs
- relevance of DoD lessons learned from handling other dangerous materials
- barriers to an effective program and recommended improvements

During the six-week course of this study, the task force was briefed by a variety of subject matter experts in the field of biological research, safety, and security, as well as laboratory directors and relevant management personnel from academia, industry, and other government organizations. In spite of the short time available to complete the study, and in accordance with the terms of reference, the task force was able to visit most of the DoD's high-containment laboratories in the continental United States (CONUS), and visited or received briefings from at least two laboratories with similar type operations in other relevant government agencies, academia, and the industrial sector.

Based on these visits and supplementing briefings, as well as the experience of the task force members, the task force considered the potential threat scenarios and the likelihood of accidental or intentional misuse of BSATs. The task force members formulated a series of principal findings and associated recommendations as summarized below. The single overarching finding is:

> **A determined adversary cannot be prevented from obtaining very dangerous biological materials intended for nefarious purposes, if not from DoD labs, then from other sources. The best we can do is to make it more difficult. We need to recognize this reality and be prepared to mitigate the effects of a biological attack. We, as a nation, are not prepared.**

Findings

- The task force found the safety and security programs in the DoD facilities they assessed to be as good or better than those in comparably sized facilities in other government, industry, and academic sectors:

    - DoD regulations exceed those imposed by the Center for Disease Control and Prevention (CDC).

    - This finding is based on briefings, interviews, and observations, but without any direct means to observe actual practices.

    - Several of the new non-DoD Biological Safety Level (BSL) labs are more modern than the DoD labs, and if the U. S. Army Medical Research Institute of Infectious Diseases (USAMRIID) is to stay in the forefront and address evolving threats, investment in new infrastructure must be of a sufficient level.

- A strong safety record of the laboratories is a good indicator of the general effectiveness of safety measures.

- Safety and security require substantial investment. Research programs cannot bear this cost.

- The "isolated" computer system could represent a serious vulnerability but the task force did not have the resources to verify this.

- The insider threat dominates internal security concerns:

  - An insider could probably transfer BSAT out of the facility or supply chain without being discovered, regardless of defensive countermeasures. One can only make it difficult and uncertain for the insider.

  - Detection of an insider threat is difficult even with extensive monitoring of the emotional and mental state of BSAT-certified employees, including transport personnel.

- Improved video monitoring of labs can be superior to the two-person rule for detecting or deterring nefarious activities in the lab and can be valuable in assuring good safety practices.

- BSAT transport works well today using the "lost in the crowd" approach, and may be worse with a two-person rule.

- Inspections are needed, but are currently burdensome (too many, different guidelines, lack of expertise, etc.) and should be improved.

- Advancing technology is increasing ease of terrorist access to dangerous pathogens worldwide, making it urgent to support the long-term development of broad-spectrum diagnostics, therapeutics, vaccines, and consequence management capabilities.

- Rather than steal BSAT from a DoD lab, other paths would appear preferable for an adversary (*e.g.*, natural sources, non-DoD labs, non-U.S. labs, genomic synthesis) except possibly in the case of a blackmailed or disgruntled employee working from the inside.

- DoD should avoid those measures that are significantly detrimental to the laboratory mission, onerous, or detract from morale unless the measure significantly improves security or safety.

- Covert external threats are unlikely and layers of defensive measures serve to deter further.

- An external "attack" by a demonstration mob or explosives, coupled with inflammatory media, could panic the surrounding populace.

- Public education now is the best way to mitigate public panic later, if there is a loss or perceived loss of containment.

The task force addressed the DoD's biological safety and security program from an end-to-end perspective in order to assess the proper balance of policies, regulations, and challenges in conducting BSAT research. The following seven recommendations capture the broad essence of the study; however, the main report contains further detail as to why these recommendations were chosen and the specifics of their execution.

Recommendations

#1 Cyber Red Team

- Red team the computer systems at USAMRIID (and, depending on the results, other DoD labs) to seek potential access through external connections or a malevolent insider.

- A different team, familiar with lab functionality, should determine what actions a malefactor might be able to do with full access to site computers and develop a plan for mitigating this risk.

#2 Monitoring Activities

- Make minor changes to monitor activities in labs to improve effectiveness without introducing significantly obtrusive measures that are unwarranted by the threat.

- Hold annual meetings of all Biological Personnel Reliability Program (BPRP) personnel to reinforce values, moral obligations, and observations that ought to be reported.

#3 Biological Personnel Reliability Program

- Maintain use of the BPRP tailored to bio-defense work; balance risk from malevolent insider against detriment to laboratory mission.

#4 OCONUS Regulations

- Issue a blanket waiver for use of Department of State background investigations (conducted by U.S. Embassy Regional Security Office), in place of National Agency Check with Local Agency Check and Credit (NACLC), among host country personnel working with BSATs in DoD labs outside the continental United States (OCONUS).

- Grant waiver authority on shipments to laboratory commanders to determine minimum security measures based on local risk assessment and conditions for which shipments must occur (*e.g.*, public health, forensic analysis).

#5 *Compliance Inspections*

- Provide resources for an independent inspection team of authoritative and successful individuals, and work toward a single inspection team for all DoD laboratories.

#6 *BSAT Transport*

- Review use of the two-person rule for BSAT shipments; threat is unlikely.

- Continue to use "lost in the crowd" approach used for the shipments involving DoD labs.

- As a future option, investigate potential of flight safe, tamper-resistant shipping containers.

#7 *Public Education and Relations*

- Educate the public in regions around BSAT facilities on mission, safety measures, and level of risk, to counter an attack intended to inflame the media and close the facility.

- All CONUS bio-containment facilities and their immediate senior commands within DoD should develop a risk communication plan, a public relations plan, and a media portion to any emergency response plans.

In summary, the recommendations in these seven areas will enhance current bio-safety and bio-security operations at the DoD laboratories while minimizing the impact of regulatory processes on the missions of those laboratories. The cost of implementing these recommendations is believed to be modest, but should not be imposed on the research programs that affect the missions of the labs.

Chapter 1. Introduction

Background

Since renouncing the development, production, stockpiling, and use of biological weapons in 1969, the Department of Defense (DoD) has invested in militarily relevant biological defense. Also in 1969, the U.S. Army Medical Research Institute of Infectious Diseases (USAMRIID) was created to develop medical defensive countermeasures. Medical biological defensive research has focused mainly on the development of vaccines, drugs, and diagnostics as defensive countermeasures.

DoD maintains a network of laboratories and centers dedicated to developing defensive capabilities to protect against biological select agents and toxins (BSATs). Most of these facilities evolved from small specialized laboratories that focused on a particular area of today's modern research and development—performing work that ranges from basic science and technology to supporting systems in biological defense. All laboratories participating in DoD research, development, test, and evaluation (RDT&E) are required to comply with the code of federal regulations and DoD directives, policies, and regulations. These sets of regulations specify safety and security policy, responsibilities, and procedures for service and contract laboratories conducting research and development in support of the DoD biological defense program.

In general, biosafety encompasses risk assessment, safe practices, and containment equipment to protect researchers from exposure to infectious agents and facility barrier systems that prevent the release of an agent into the environment to ensure protection of the public health. Biosecurity includes physical security, select agent accountability, and personnel reliability in an effort to prevent unauthorized access to biological select agents and toxins. There is obvious overlap between the two terms. The DoD labs employ an in-depth approach to securing BSATs during operations that require manipulation, storage, or transport of these hazardous materials. Layers of security include physical security of facilities, secured storage equipment, secured transportation of BSATs, surveillance systems, and personnel security processes that assure only the most reliable and skilled personnel have access to the materials necessary to conduct research appropriate to the mission.[1]

There are numerous directives and regulations, established by different government agencies that govern biological safety and security (see list of References and Regulations at the end of this report).

Origins of the Study and Terms of Reference

Recent concerns and events have drawn attention to issues surrounding laboratory safety and security—not the least of which was the identification of Dr. Bruce Ivins, a DoD employee and a scientist at USAMRIID, as the suspected perpetrator behind the "anthrax letters" mailed in 2001. In an attempt to prevent a recurrence of such an event in the future, the Under Secretary of Defense for Acquisition, Technology, and Logistics (USD (AT&L)), with support of the secretaries of the three military departments, asked the chairman of the Defense Science Board to charter a task force to take a fresh look at biological safety and security. The task force was charted to examine the current status of the safety, security, and personnel reliability programs of the DoD biological defense labs compared with other similar operations in academia, industry, and the federal government, and to make recommendations for improvements in the DoD program. The study focused on DoD, academia, industry, and other government agencies' biological research and development laboratories that use BSATs. The basic tasks to be undertaken were:

- Assess the adequacy of current and proposed policies.

- Evaluate the use and storage of BSATs, meeting stringent standards for safety, security, and personnel reliability.

- Compare similar operations between DoD and other government, academia, and industry labs.

---

1. In 2004, DoD Directive (DoDD) 5210.88, Safeguarding Biological Select Agents and Toxins, established security policy and assigned responsibilities for safeguarding BSATs. In 2005, the Department of Health and Human Services (HHS) published the final rule for 42 CFR 73, whereas the U.S. Department of Agriculture (USDA) published the final rules for 7 CFR 331 and 9 CFR 121. The Army Regulation (AR) 50-1, Biological Surety, final version, was implemented in October 2008. In addition, minimum security standards for safeguarding BSATs are covered by DoD 5210.89, AR 190-17, OPNAVINST 5530.16, and DODI 5210.89_AFI 10-3901. Each of the military departments implemented these policies, directives, regulations, and memoranda to comply as appropriate. All of the above documents apply to military laboratories and civilian contractors (especially BSATs received from DoD) supporting DoD biological defense research programs.

- Determine the relevance of DoD lessons learned from handling other dangerous materials.
- Identify barriers to an effective program and recommend improvements.

Study Execution

The study investigation was limited to a total of six weeks by the required coordination with other related activities. With limited time, the task force devoted its time and energy visiting most of the DoD labs in the continental United States (CONUS) and visited or received briefings from at least two laboratories operated within each of three other sectors: other government agencies, academia, and industry. In addition, they sought to gain perspective on BSATs by understanding the breakdown of procedures in prior incidents such as those at Texas A&M University[2] and Boston University.[3]

Table 1 lists the organizations that were visited or provided briefings. The right three columns provide some perspective on size and scope, as these factors make a difference in procedures and practices. The Galveston BSL-4 lab of the University of Texas Medical Branch was still recovering from the damage caused by Hurricane Ike and therefore did not provide a briefing or allow a visit by task force members. However, two of the task force members visited the senior management of the university and discussed their perspective on operations in Galveston.

---

2. Center for Disease Control and Prevention (CDC) report dated August 31, 2007. Subject: Texas A&M University: Report of site visit.
3. Boston Public Health Commission report dated March 28, 2005. Subject: Report of Pneumonic Tularemia in Three Boston University Researchers.

Table 1. BSAT Site Visits and Briefings

Category	Organization	Task Force Visit or Brief	Size of BSAT Lab*	BSAT Agents	BSAT-certified Persons
DoD					
	USAMRIID	Visit	Large	51	306
	WRAIR/NMRC	Visit	Medium	15	33
	Cairo	Brief	Small	4	4
	Lima	Brief	Small	6	7
	Bangkok	Brief	Small	0	0
	ECBC (Edgewood)	Visit	Small	30	99
	WDTC (Dugway)	Brief	Medium	19	33
	711 HPW (Brooks City Base)	Brief	Small	2	12
	Dahlgren NSWC	Brief	Small	2	7
Other Government					
	CDC	Visit	Large	60	833
	NBACC (DHS)	Brief	Not operational		
	NIAID (NIH)	Visit	Large	13	200
Industry					
	Battelle (BBRC)	Brief	Large	341	230
	MRI	Brief	Large	15	62
	SWFBR	Visit	Medium	35	60
Academia					
	Boston University (NEIDL)**	Brief	Medium	16	17
	Georgia State University	Visit	Small	1	5
	UTMB (Galveston National Laboratory)	See text	Large	36	372

*Large: 15 or more labs/suites; Medium: 5-14 labs/suites; Small: 1-4 labs/suites.

**Not operational at the time of this study.

During on-site visits to the laboratories and briefings from those not visited, the task force probed a variety of issues and topics. Limitations of time did not permit comprehensive assessment but typical subjects covered during visits and briefings included the following:

- organization structure and overview
- Biological Select Agent and Toxin Program
- BSAT facilities and operations
- BSAT security program

- perimeter and internal security systems

- floor plans and lab layouts

- cyber systems and controls

- Biological Personnel Reliability Program (BPRP) (enrollment and medical certification)—monitoring emotional variations

- biosecurity program structure—certifying official, surety officers, monitors

- BSAT accountability—inventory control, documentation, record keeping, computer systems, software used

- audits/inspections—usefulness, outcome, and actions taken; deficiencies reported in past three years

- challenges, issues, concerns

The task force faced a number of limitations in trying to satisfy the terms of reference. As a result, principal caveats include the following:

- Factors examined lack quantitative measures so that conclusions relied primarily on experience and judgment of panel members.

- Policies and procedures may not represent actual practices, particularly over an extended time. The task force did not observe actual practices.

- Tradeoffs between cost and mission performance on one hand and improvements in safety and security on the other were considered by the task force, and should be taken into consideration by the decision makers before implementing changes to current policies and practices.

- Safety and security often overlap; the distinction in this report is arbitrary. For example, video monitoring of a lab often serves both.

Biological Select Agents and Toxins and Bio-Safety Level Laboratories

After the terrorist attacks on September 11, 2001 and the anthrax letters mailed later that same year, Congress recognized the threat of terrorism and enacted the USA Patriot Act in 2001. The Patriot Act makes it illegal for an individual to possess BSATs for any reason other than bona fide research. The act states: "Whoever knowingly possesses any biological agent, toxin, or delivery system of a type or in a quantity that, under the circumstances, is not reasonably justified by a prophylactic, protective, bona fide research, or other peaceful purpose." In response to these events, DoD and the service Inspector General teams inspected DoD biological RDT&E laboratories and advocated development of a surety program for biological agents, similar to existing surety programs for nuclear and chemical programs. In 2002, Congress enacted the Public Health Security and Bioterrorism Preparedness and Response Act that tasked the Department of Health and Human Services (HHS) and the U.S. Department of Agriculture (USDA) to prepare a list of select agents and toxins based on the criteria specified in the act; the current version of that list is found in Table 2 along with the associated bio-safety levels (BSL).[4]

Table 3 lists all of the BSL-4 labs in North America that are either currently operational or under construction, including one Canadian lab. It also lists the additional DoD labs that function at BSL-3. This study focused primarily on the labs listed in Table 3. A short description of many of these labs can be found in Appendix A of this report.

---

4. BSL are discussed in detail in Chapter 2.

Table 2. Biological Select Agents and Toxins

BSL-4

Viruses

• **Cercophithecine herpesvirus 1 (Herpes B)	• Kyasanur Forest disease	• Russian Spring-Summer encephalitis
• Crimean-Congo hemorrhagic fever	• Lassa fever virus	• Sabia
• Ebola	• Machupo	• Variola major (Smallpox)
• Tick-borne encephalitis complex (flavi)	• Marburg	• Variola minor (Alastrim)
• Guanarito	• Nipah	
• Hendra	• Omsk hemorrhagic fever	
• Kumlinge (Cent Eur. TBE)		

BSL-3

Bacteria

• Bacillus anthracis	• *Clostridium Perfringens epsilon	• Mycoplasma mycoides mycoides (contagious bovine pleuropneumonia)
• Brucella abortus	• *Francisella tularensis	• *Rickettsia prowazekii
• Brucella suis	• Mycoplasma capricolum (contagious caprine pleuropneumonia)	• *Rickettsia rickettsii
• Burkholderia mallei		• *Yersinia pestis
• Brucella melitensis		
• Burkholderia pseudomallei		

Viruses

• African horse sickness	• ***Far Eastern Tick-Borne Encephalitis	• Menangle
• African swine fever	• Flexal	• *Monkeypox
• Akabane	• Foot and Mouth Disease	• Newcastle Disease (exotic)
• Avian Influenza	• Goat pox	• Peste des petits ruminants
• Blue tongue (exotic)	• *Influenza virus non-contemporary	• Rift Valley fever
• Bovine Spongiform Encephalopathy	• *Influenza virus pandemic 1918	• Rinderpest
• Camel pox virus	• *Japanese encephalitis	• Swine Vesicular Disease
• Central European Tick-Borne Encephalitis	• Junin	• Venezuelan equine encephalitis
• Classical Swine Fever	• Lumpy Skin Disease	• *Vesicular stomatitis (Exotic)
• ***Eastern Equine Encephalitis	• Malignant Catarrhal Fever	

Fungal Agents | Toxins

• *Coccidioides immitis	• *Abrin	• *Staphylococcal enterotoxins
• *Coccoidiodes posadasii	• *Botulinum neurotoxins of clostridium	

BSL-2

Toxins

• Conotoxins	• Shiga-like ribosome inactivating proteins	• T-2 Toxin
• Ricin	• Tetrodotoxin	
• Saxitoxin	• Shigatoxin	

*Depending on usage is categorized as BSL-2 or BSL-3.

**Depending on usage, can be categorized as BSL-2, BSL-3, or BSL-4.

***Depending on usage these are categorized as BSL-3 or BSL-4.

Note: Table 2 is a list of HHS and USDA Biological Select Agents and Toxins, as part of 7 CFR Part 331, 9 CFR Part 121, and 42 CFR 73. Revised on 11-17-2008.

Table 3. North America BSL-4 and DoD BSL-3/4 Labs with BSAT

BSL-4 Labs (North America)	DoD BSL-3/4 Labs with BSAT

Operational Labs
· Centers for Disease Control and Prevention, Atlanta, GA
· USAMRIID, Frederick, MD
· Southwest Foundation for Biomedical Research, San Antonio, TX
· University of Texas Medical Branch, Galveston, TX
· Georgia State University, Atlanta, GA
· Health Canada, Winnipeg, Canada
Under Construction Labs
· National Biodefense Analysis and CM CTR, DHS
· Integrated Research Facility, NIH
· Rocky Mountain Labs (NIH), Hamilton, MT
· National Emerging Infectious Disease Laboratory, Boston University, Boston, MA
	· Naval Medical Research Center, Silver Spring, MD*
	· Walter Reed Army Institute of Research, Silver Spring, MD*
	· Edgewood Chemical and Biological Center, Aberdeen Proving Ground (APG), MD
	· Army Medical Research Institute of Chemical Defense, APG, MD
	· Dahlgren Naval Surface Warfare Center, Dahlgren, VA
	· West Desert Test Center, Dugway Proving Ground, UT
	· 711th Human Performance Wing/RHPC, Brooks City Base, San Antonio, TX
	· Armed Forces Institute of Pathology, Washington, D.C.
	· OCONUS:
	  - Bangkok, Thailand: US Army Medical Component of the Armed Forces Research Institute of the Medical Sciences (AFIRMS)
	  - Cairo, Egypt: Naval Medical Research Unit Three (NAMRU-3)
	  - Lima, Peru: Naval Medical Research Center Detachment (NMRCD)
	*These labs are co-located.

To provide some measure of the scope and scale of BSAT work in the United States, there are a total of 324 BSAT entities (*e.g.,* labs and centers) according to the Centers for Disease Control and Prevention (CDC) and, as of April 2008, about 14,000 people were approved for BSAT access (9,918 by CDC and 4,336 by USDA APHIS[5]). These numbers include support personnel and those who have limited access to BSAT. In fact, since the program's inception, a total of 28,593 requests for personnel access have been processed. A small number of the requests were disapproved (158) and of those disapproved, 51 were appealed with 30 sustained and 21 overturned.

---

5. Animal and Plant Health Inspection Service.

Chapter 2. Biological Safety

Biological safety (or biosafety) is primarily the application of concepts relating to risk assessment, personal protective equipments, engineering controls, policies, and preventive measures to promote safe laboratory practices, procedures, and the proper use of containment equipment and facilities. In biological research, laboratory scientists and technicians apply these concepts to prevent laboratory-acquired infections and the release of pathogenic organisms into the environment. The Biosafety in Microbiological and Biomedical Laboratories (BMBL)[6] manual is considered a cornerstone of biosafety practice and policy written by the National Institutes of Health (NIH) and CDC in the United States. The basic principles relate to containment and risk assessment. Containment includes the microbiological practices, procedures, safety equipment, and facility safeguards that protect laboratory workers, the environment, and the public from exposure to infectious micro-organisms that are handled and stored in the laboratory. The risk assessment is the process by which appropriate microbial practices, safety equipment, and facility safeguards are selected to prevent laboratory-associated infections.

The BMBL is considered a "safety bible." It is used by all U.S. laboratories, including those under DoD, other government agencies, academia, and industrial laboratories that presented to, or were visited by, the task force. It is also used in many institutions worldwide.

The primary risk criteria used to define the four ascending levels of containment known as biosafety levels 1 through 4 are infectivity, severity of disease, transmissibility, and the nature of work being conducted. Each level of containment describes the microbiological practices, safety equipment, and facility safeguards for the corresponding level of risk associated with handling a particular agent. Biosafety level 1 (BSL-1) is the basic level of protection and is appropriate for agents that are not known to cause disease in normal, healthy humans. Biosafety level 2 (BSL-2) is appropriate for handling moderate-risk agents that

---

6. The BMBL is used at HHS, NIH, and CDC, among other government institutions. *Biosafety in Microbiological and Biomedical Laboratories (BMBL) 5th Edition.* U.S. Department of Health and Human Services Centers for Disease Control and Prevention, and National Institutes of Health. Fifth Edition, Feb 2007. U.S. Government Printing Office, Washington, D.C.: 2007.

cause human disease of varying severity by ingestion or through percutaneous or mucous membrane exposure. Biosafety level 3 (BSL-3) is appropriate for agents with a known potential for aerosol transmission, that may cause serious and potentially lethal infections, and that are indigenous or exotic in origin. Exotic agents that pose a high individual risk of life-threatening disease by infectious aerosols, and for which no treatment is available, are restricted to high containment laboratories that meet strict biosafety level 4 (BSL-4) standards.

Figure 1 illustrates the typical layout of a containment laboratory. The typical floor plan of a BSL-3/BSL-4 lab suite includes a containment area (red), entry and preparation area (blue), and an office area (yellow). Personnel access the containment area through the chemical shower (CHSH). Entrance to the BSL suite is through the area on the bottom right corner called change room. As shown, the containment area is isolated and comprises laboratory space, animal rooms, necropsy room, equipment room (EQPT), and double-door autoclaves (labeled as A). The double-door autoclaves ensure that all materials from the containment area are sterilized before they leave the facility. The associated office area is normally located outside the containment area as shown in the upper left hand corner.

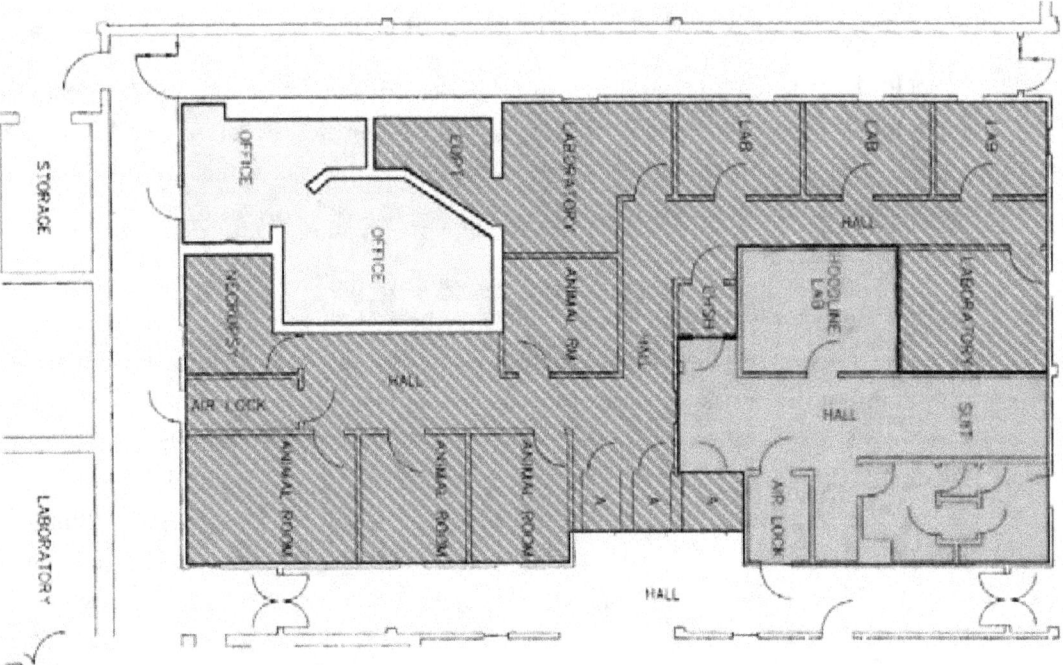

Figure 1. Typical BSL-4 and BSL-3 Lab Floor Plan

Biosafety ensures that operations with BSAT are conducted in a safe, secure, and reliable manner to protect workers, as well as the public, from unintended exposure to infectious pathogens. As mentioned earlier, the various layers of a biosafety program may include assessing individual carefulness, physical barriers, personal protective equipment, safety training and mentorship, risk management, area surveillance of labs and occupational health screening. Risk assessment is the primary responsibility of the principal investigators and the directors of the laboratories. For example, the supervisor of each person working in the laboratory conducts a detailed specific workplace risk assessment. Table 4 shows some of the factors used at USAMRIID for assessing the safety risks.[7]

Table 4. Select Safety Factors Used at USAMRIID

USAMRIID Safety Factors	
• Negative pressure/HEPA filtration	• Suite-specific plans
• Steam sterilized water waste	• Radioisotope safety
• Data-based training systems	• Redundant power systems
• Double-door autoclaves	• Compressed air tank farm for suits
• Positive pressure suits	• Backup generators for maintaining pressure differential
• Proper secondary containment for aerosols	• Special immunization program
• Chemical hygiene plans	• Equipment calibration program
• Emergency operation plans	
• Composite risk management	

Typical risks of concern for personnel exposure include needle stick or scalpel accident, bite from an infected animal, attenuated agent contaminated with pathogenic agent, medical failure to diagnose lab infection, and deviation from approved practices. The risk of release of pathogens to the environment requires a layered containment typically including practices and procedures, safety equipment (*e.g.*, HEPA-filtered biosafety cabinets), facility design and

---

7. The risk assessment begins with a detailed analysis of the various tasks intended to be performed within the laboratory and is evaluated in terms of potential exposure to the infectious agent or BSAT. Consideration includes use of sharp objects or handling animals that can potentially result in puncture injuries, equipment generating aerosols, etc. Once the hazards are identified, risk mitigation can be accomplished by isolating the operations or substituting with engineering controls, such as biological safety cabinets, sealed equipment, containment cages for animals, negative pressure, air treatment systems, and High Efficiency Particulate Air (HEPA) filters among others. Other personal protective equipment could be used to protect against contact, mucosal, and respiratory exposures. The layers of containment in a laboratory consist of a combination of factors that include risk assessment, practices, and procedures, followed by safety equipment for personal protection, facility design, and engineering controls and decontamination procedures.

engineering controls (*e.g.*, ventilation systems, air treatment systems and positive pressure), and decontamination procedures. Plans are also put in place, and must be executed in a timely manner, to prevent contamination outside of the lab that may result from natural causes—such as a hurricane or other natural disaster—or malicious acts. For example, when Hurricane Ike was certain to strike Galveston, UTMB euthanized and destroyed all infected animals.[8]

The task force received information regarding the inspection regime of the DoD facilities. The laboratories underwent numerous inspections due to the various regulatory and licensing requirements. The task force focused on the safety inspections conducted by CDC and the military departments. CDC conducts comprehensive inspections with an experienced team at every facility engaged in BSAT work. Moreover, the CDC inspection team is comprised of experienced individuals who are able to maintain proficiency because of the large number of facilities and resultant inspections, even though the CDC inspects each laboratory every three years.

In comparison, the DoD inspection teams are beginning to acquire similar expertise. Due to the small number of DoD facilities (8) and the inspection periodicity staggered to complement the CDC inspection schedule, DoD inspection teams would inspect on less than a monthly basis. Since each service inspected its own laboratory, the inspection periodicity was much less than one per month. The DoD inspection teams generally did not include a microbiologist, so expertise was gained via course completion. Course completion does not substitute for the experience and expertise gained by individuals who successfully complete a tour of duty in a facility. (The more rigorous and operationally focused DoD inspection teams are comprised of personnel who successfully complete prior tours of duty in that particular area. Tours of duty on these inspection teams are considered advantageous and provide higher rates of promotion than many other career paths). Inspection results were not shared between laboratories, which did not allow any lessons learned approach to self-improvement.

---

8. "Biosafety Lab Passes Disaster Test," *Nature* Vol 455; October 23, 2008, p. 1012.

Safety Findings

Safety policies used in DoD labs appear effective but the following steps would add value to current policies:

- Improve inspections by creating a single team that conducts all DoD inspections. This team should be comprised of authoritative and successful individuals with expertise in microbiology. The inspections could be more deliberate (longer) but less intrusive, *e.g.*, through better use of video recordings to determine weaknesses in actual practices.

- Provide a central, accessible database for significant discrepancies and lessons learned, such as the incidents at Texas A&M University and Boston University.

- Follow-up personnel absences from work due to medical reasons to help correlate medical care outside the lab.

- Emphasize safety culture as the most important asset.

Chapter 3. Security

For the purposes of this study, the main objective of biosecurity is to properly safeguard BSATs and prevent loss, theft, diversion, or unauthorized access or use of a DoD laboratory. The primary concerns of the task force were the malicious threats of either those attempting to seize BSAT material for their own use, or those intent on destroying the lab or its containment, such as to terrorize a regional population. It is clear that one cannot stop all determined attacks but a well-layered defense can make an attack so difficult that the attacker will turn to an easier target, of which there are many.

Spectrum of Threats

Table 5 lists the task force-selected spectrum of varying attacker motivations and objectives, the threats to achieve these objectives, a subjective assessment of the vulnerability, and the rationale for that assessment. Derived from this table, the following threats were considered by the task force:

- physical attack to destroy buildings/close the lab

- physical mob attack, such as animal rights extremists bent on "making a statement" and/or releasing animals

- cyber attack against access controls, environmental controls, transport plans, inventory, etc.

- insider attack ranging from stealing BSAT for terrorist use, employee being blackmailed or under financial stress being forced to operate on behalf of terrorists, or a disgruntled employee

Table 5. Security Threat Scenarios

Example Security Threats			
Adversary Motive	**Potential Threats**	**Relative Likelihood**	**Rationale**
Physical Make a statement for some cause; *e.g.*, animal rights	Mob breach defenses and enter building, *e.g.*, to release animals and then accept arrest by responding force	**Medium–Low**	More likely at less protected facilities than those of DoD. Could use explosives to pass access controls
BSAT destruction	Paramilitary attack to seize BSAT stocks	**Very Low**	Paramilitary attack is open combat and would be opposed quickly by superior forces
BSAT destruction and populace terrorized	Air explosives delivery (in some cases truck where there are no truck barriers)	**Very Low**	Probably low on terrorist list of iconic targets for 9-11 type attack
Cyber BSAT destruction	Cyber attack on lab systems or supporting infrastructure	**Medium**	Likely non-attributable
Steal BSAT	Outsider entering; supported by cyber access control	**Very Low**	Much more complex operation. Likely to trigger immediate response
Steal BSAT	Holding insider's family hostage to force bringing out BSAT	**Low**	Difficult to ascertain that getting right material
Insider Steal BSAT	Insider theft	**Medium**	Covert theft, ‑weaponize" elsewhere. Seed stock available through less risky routes

Physical Threat

Physical attacks are unlikely for labs that are located on military bases where the perimeter and entry protection are typical and probably sufficient to divert attackers to less risky targets. While the task force did not inspect for other than the obvious physical protection, the General Accountability Office (GAO) conducted such an inspection in September 2008.[9] This independent inspection covered only external physical barriers and with criteria well in excess of CDC physical security standards (Table 6). The GAO physical security standards made little reference to the threat. Their conclusion: "Other examples of more stringent regulations for BSL-4 labs include those of military labs that also follow far stricter DoD physical security requirements. For example, lab A [identified by knowledgeable individuals as USAMRIID] had several layers of security, including a perimeter security fence and roving patrol of armed guards, visible inside and outside the perimeter fence." It should be noted that some labs meeting only 3–4 of the GAO criteria, were, quite properly, fully approved by CDC.

Table 6. GAO: External Physical Security Inspection Criteria

GAO Inspection Criteria
· Outer-tiered perimeter boundary
· Blast stand-off area (between lab and perimeter barriers)
· Barriers to prevent vehicles from approaching lab
· Loading docks located outside footprint of main building
· Exterior windows do not provide direct access to the lab
· Command and control center
· Closed circuit TV (CCTV) monitored by command and control center
· Active intrusion detection system integrated with CCTV
· Camera coverage for all exterior lab building entrances
· Perimeter lighting of complex
· Visible armed guard presence at all public entrances to lab
· Roving armed guard patrols of perimeter
· X-ray magnetometer machines in operation at building entrances
· Vehicle screening
· Visitor screening

9. GAO Report to Congressional Committees. *Biosafety Laboratories: Perimeter Security Assessment of the Nation's Five BSL-4 Laboratories.* Washington: Government Accountability Office, 2008. (GAO-08-1092).

Cyber Threat

None of the labs appears to have adequately considered the cyber threat. Some indicated that their critical computer systems were "isolated." The task force did not believe that any of the computer systems should be considered as truly isolated. The computers that control access systems are obviously wired throughout the complex connecting key pads, lock controls, and the like. Every piece of modern equipment will have its own computer(s). At least two of the non-DoD labs had either wireless or remote-wired access.

Beyond that, during installation or maintenance it would not be difficult to add connections if that is even necessary, and there is always the possibility of malware (malicious circuits in the hardware) or malicious software from the supply chain. The task force did not have the time or resources to properly investigate these concerns but believe doing so is important.

The following illustrates some examples of the scenarios of possible concern if an adversary were able to penetrate the system and manipulate the control systems:

- An insider could manipulate the access control system (ACS) to allow access to unauthorized persons or remove access for authorized persons.

- Another function carried out by the ACS is to log entry and exit from different access points in the system. The logs provide useful forensic evidence of an individual's location during periods of interest. An insider may be able to manipulate the logs, which could hide the presence of an individual in different parts of the complex.

- A knowledgeable insider (*e.g.*, ACS IT support) may have sufficient opportunity to perform the above during the normal course of his or her duties. An individual who may not possess the same access to the ACS may also choose to connect the ACS to an external network and enable exploitation of the ACS from outside the confines of the lab by a knowledgeable individual. For example, a network coexists within USAMRIID, which is designed and configured to allow access to the Internet. At the Naval Medical Research Center (NMRC) facility, the ACS included a remote alarm monitoring capability, which meant some part of its ACS travels outside the confines of its building.

- The USAMRIID building management system is reported as a standalone system. Manipulation of this system could disable all environmental factors (*e.g.*, negative pressure) used to ensure containment. The system is reported to have several monitor points that are used for infrastructure monitoring. These access points are potential vulnerabilities awaiting exploitation.

- The task force heard from a large facility that allows infrastructure monitoring by individuals from their homes. Penetration of any external portion of the network could allow manipulation of the facilities' infrastructure.

In summary, the task force concluded that the isolated computer system may not be "isolated" because of apparent connectivity to the rest of the laboratory complex, but did not have the resources or time to investigate this potential. Instead, the task force recommended that independent cyber security professionals from the National Security Agency (NSA) or the Army Information Operations group be directed to thoroughly probe this possibility. At the same time, those familiar with the labs and their technical and administrative functioning should conduct an analysis of what harm could be done by someone with full access to the site computer systems.

Insider Threat

There was general agreement that an insider could remove BSAT material without detection. However, there was also considerable skepticism that an insider could use a DoD laboratory to proceed with weaponization steps undetected, other than in cases where the planned legitimate work involved equipment or processes that might enable weaponization; in such cases, additional security measures and monitoring should be provided and carefully observed.

The task force considered the timeframes and motivations of an insider attempting to steal or release BSAT and concluded that there are four potential classes of threat:

- **Terrorists** with a long-planned event operating on an extended time scale. The likelihood in this case is that the malefactor would go for an easier source than a DoD lab unless they had a well-placed insider.

- **Domestic terrorists** intent on shutting down the lab, such as an animal rights group with a sympathetic insider.

- **Insider under terrorist control** who is being blackmailed or is in serious financial stress, or whose family is being held hostage.

- **Disgruntled employee** determined to undertake a random-victim attack.

Each of these cases provides different challenges for those concerned with security.

Attempting to manipulate large quantities of agents (or weaponization) with steps that require specific equipment (*e.g.*, lyophilizers) is much more likely to arouse suspicion and be detected by an alert management. On the other hand, these further steps (weaponization and quantity) could be accomplished in a garage, basement, or a less-protected lab, such as in a school, with some risk to persons nearby. Any individual who intends to employ a pathogen as a weapon is unlikely to be inhibited from using makeshift facilities that lack the full suite of safety practices utilized by the biodefense labs.

In the case of a disgruntled or stressed employee, the detection problem is to detect the action that hides such a vial on the lab worker or notes his or her emotional state. Even more difficult to detect would be the worker who either intentionally injects himself or herself with the pathogen or hides a small amount on their person which could be cultured once it was smuggled outside the containment area.

Potential improvements considered against the insider threat include increased and enhanced video monitoring of the labs, augmented Biological Personnel Reliability Program, two-person rule in the labs, and heightened management attention. The goal of these defenses should be to cause the malefactor to go elsewhere to obtain the desired pathogens, thus reducing the risk of insider threat even lower at DoD labs.

Two-person Rule and Video Monitoring

The current view on thwarting an attempt to steal weaponizable BSATs is typically to apply a two-person rule for working in the lab. In addition, most labs have some degree of video monitoring with a bank of display screens at some central point (*e.g.*, guard post). The two-person rule is considered onerous, and potentially dangerous as it requires someone other than the active scientist to be present in the lab. It is also costly in terms of dollars and personnel. The video monitor is typically thought of as a forensic tool after the fact, but in real time it is only a bank of screens occasionally observed by people who are not experts in lab techniques. Table 7 outlines some of the pros and cons of the two approaches. The task force judged neither approach to be effective as they are used today. Even as a forensic tool, the video is generally retained for short periods of time and the need for forensics may occur months or years after the theft.

Table 7. Detecting Ill-Intent Through Observation

	Cameras	Two-Person Rule
Who	**Pro:** Captures everyone in suite and correlates ID with entry code and time. Relatively benign to staff. **Con:** Requires someone with knowledge to monitor or review images	**Pro:** Directs focus to likely insider threats. Enhances safety and emergency response. **Con:** Requires significant restructuring and or scheduling of staff. Only modestly deters theft of seed material. Majority of staff are not a threat but will be treated as such.
When	**Pro:** Continuous coverage—some camera systems are only activated when entry has occurred **Con:** Data overload when looking for an unspecified event such as theft of a vial or self-infection	**Pro:** Coverage only when suite entry required. **Con:** The malefactor accompanied by a second person can readily observe where the escort is looking.
What	**Pro:** Tool that could prevent weaponization of BSAT in the DoD laboratory. Does help with emergency response and safety issues. **Con:** Will create additional bureaucracy to differentiate between legitimate and suspicious activities. Low likelihood to detecting BSAT theft.	**Pro:** Very likely to detect unique preparation of biological agents thereby deterring use of government facilities. Reduces bureaucracy to monitor legitimacy of activity. **Con:** Collusion would render this countermeasure ineffective. Would not likely prevent theft of seed biological material even without collusion.
Why	**Pro:** Looks good to the uninformed (*i.e.*, public). Meets part of current biosecurity regulatory intent. **Con:** Costs a lot of money for hardware, storage and or review. Low likelihood of agent theft detection.	**Pro:** Makes some illicit activities more difficult. Meets some current ―industry standards.‖ **Con:** Costs a lot of money and impacts scientific enterprise and moral by treating everyone a suspect. Second person unlikely to be ―productive‖ during observation duties.
Other Implications	In general, cameras have a deterrent effect. However, without specific procedural knowledge a film reviewer/monitor would likely not understand what they were viewing. Storage (even with digital) becomes problematic and costly.	Significant impact on scientific enterprise. Every lab and lab procedure will require redundant available staff up to four persons for each procedure and lab location to ensure coverage. This will increase enrollments in BPRP, Special Immunization Program, occupational heath, etc.

With respect to monitoring lab work to detect nefarious activities, the task force concluded the following:

- The two-person rule for security has many disadvantages but may be effective in certain, limited circumstances, primarily for safety while working with highly pathogenic materials or laboratory animals.

- In the long run, costs associated with the two-person approach are excessive and the effectiveness for security is highly questionable.

- Surveillance with the two-person rule is not likely to be continuous over an extended period and a perpetrator can know when he is not being observed (the other person's back is turned). (See Figure 1 for an example of a typical lab floor plan). In addition, most labs have very constrained working areas and the observer would not be in a position to continuously observe the worker.

- Video surveillance of the labs can be much more effective than the two-person rule if enhanced with better procedures, better tools for monitoring, longer retention of recordings, and management participation. In addition, it probably results in lower long-term cost.

- Video has the advantage of constant surveillance; the malefactor doesn't know when he is being monitored or not.

- Data overload problem of video should be dealt with by spot checking and random supervisory audits, and with tools developed for that purpose.

- Video surveillance has potential cross-benefits in checking for adherence to safety procedures and should be seen by the staff as dominantly for that purpose

- Video recordings are usually kept for 30–45 days at most labs while others save them for up to a year. They should be kept longer.

Video monitoring of labs for security is preferred over the two-person rule and could be much more effective than it is today. The primary concern is the disgruntled or stressed employee and the combination of video monitoring and BPRP should be integrated to detect such individuals.

In monitoring, whether by video or by a second person, the question is where the focus should be for detecting problems most effectively. The following are examples of possible unauthorized acts that would be indicative of malfeasance:

- intentional concealing of containers or vials

- transfer of BSAT containers through showers, locker areas, or air locks

- preparation of live, dried BSATs

- unauthorized personnel in restricted areas

- manipulation of unregistered or undocumented BSAT cultures or containers

- tampering with freezer, incubator, or pass-through window locks

- manipulating BSAT cultures outside of bio-safety cabinets or outside of approved labs

- conducting animal studies without an approved protocol

- manipulating BSATs without appropriate safety procedures or equipment

- inadequate decontamination or destruction of working BSAT cultures at study conclusion

Obtaining Pathogens

There are other paths for obtaining BSAT, rather than stealing them from a lab, with less risk or difficulty to the perpetrator. With two exceptions (*i.e.*, variola (smallpox) and 1918 influenza virus), all BSATs are naturally occurring, replicating entities and can be found in any of a variety of worldwide locations such as in their natural environments, hospitals, sick animals, and other labs. Locations of both outbreaks and laboratory sources for pathogens are freely available on the Internet.

Several countries in the Middle East have BSL-3/4 level labs and seed stocks for a variety of agents. Egypt, Iran, Israel, Jordan, Syria, and Turkey have labs and credible microbiological capabilities. Iran and Egypt have pharmaceutical industries and Iran has BSL-3/4 labs for diagnostic, public health purposes. Assets for diagnostics that include viable organisms can also provide seed stocks for producing offensive agents. It is important not to mirror-image U.S. safety procedures or weapon capabilities as a necessary requirement from other countries. In addition, one tends to think of weaponization as an efficient dispersal of the pathogen, an art that is not readily available. However, efficient dispersal is not a requirement for developing a serious threat and one can always use more to overcome deficiencies in efficiency (in contrast to nukes, if one can make one biological weapon, there is no reason he or she can't make many more). For example, highly contagious diseases can be transmitted by infected persons traveling on mass transit conveyance systems.

In addition, many pathogens can be produced using chemically synthesized RNA/DNA "made from scratch." Published genetic sequences for most known pathogens are available. This gene synthesis is a rapidly evolving technology; in the judgment of the experienced microbiologists of the task force, the current state of that technology is such that it requires technician-level capabilities and understanding, and technical barriers are reducing over time. In addition, these capabilities are not cost-prohibitive for small groups and are easily affordable for state actors.

Thus, there are at least two paths for obtaining dangerous pathogens covertly, with almost no risk of detection. It would be unlikely that anyone other than a disgruntled or black-mailed employee would steal from a DoD lab with the added risk involved.

DoD Overseas Laboratories

DoD operates several military infectious disease research laboratories in different parts of the world. These laboratories outside the continental United States (OCONUS) play an important strategic role by developing effective medical countermeasures for protection against naturally occurring infectious diseases in their endemic regions and for surveillance of naturally occurring pathogens such as the avian influenza. They are typically co-located with labs of the host nation. The laboratories work closely with host nation laboratories and are often located on or near campuses alongside host country biomedical laboratories. DoD's OCONUS laboratories are required to operate within the confines of agreements with their host nations and often employ host nation citizens to accomplish their mission.

Current and proposed DoD biological security regulations, however, compromise the ability of the OCONUS labs to work with host national and international health agencies and to deal with public health threats. Two primary limitations are:

- Requiring personnel security clearances for local national employees that exceed those required to work in the U.S. Embassy, and for which no path for adjudication has been identified.

- Restricting commercial transport of BSAT to carriers that can ensure positive control and chain of custody when no such commercial service is available at the majority of OCONUS locations.

While current DoD regulations permit OCONUS labs to apply for exemptions to specific biological security requirements that cannot be met in the overseas environment, there is no avenue for blanket exemptions for the most common of these. In practice, the process of obtaining exemptions has been so slow as to make a timely response to a pressing public health problem impossible. What is needed are regulations that recognize the qualitative differences in the CONUS biodefense mission and the OCONUS public health mission, and that prescribe biological safety and security standards proportionate to the risk.

Security Findings

Summarizing the task force conclusions on security:

- Physical security is good at DoD labs but cyber vulnerabilities deserve attention.

- The insider threat dominates security concerns because the insider could provide knowledge of laboratory layouts, access to facilities, and could steal BSAT without detection.

- Video monitoring of all labs could be much more effective in detecting ill intent with effective and continuous spot checking and longer record retention which, if so enhanced, would then be much more effective than the two-person rule.

In general, security demands multiple layers of barriers to discourage or deflect undesirable behavior, thus motivating adversaries to turn to non-DoD labs with weaker defenses, or to sources that may introduce additional intelligence (*e.g.*, DNA/RNA synthesis or isolation from natural or hospital environments).

Chapter 4. Biological Personnel Reliability Program

The Patriot Act legislatively requires all individuals with access to BSATs to undergo a formal suitability check, known as a Security Risk Assessment (SRA). The SRA checks a broad range of suitability factors to determine identifiable character traits and conduct sufficient to decide whether an individual is likely or not likely to carry out BSAT work with appropriate integrity, efficiency, and effectiveness. DoD implemented a BSAT suitability program titled the Biological Personnel Reliability Program (BPRP) that is administered at the individual command level. The BPRP is designed to supplement the national level SRA but the mechanisms used to implement the BPRP duplicate, and in some cases contradict, the suitability determinations required by the Patriot Act. These will be discussed below.

The Federal Bureau of Investigation (FBI) periodically conducts an SRA on all individuals with access to BSAT.[10] All individuals undergo an SRA upon initial application. At the time the task force was meeting, the SRA was not transferable between entities; however, recent efforts allow transfer between entities under certain conditions (entities are centers or laboratory complexes, *e.g.*, USAMRIID or Edgewood). The SRA is renewed every five years for all individuals.[11] A significant number of SRAs were processed since the inception of this program (~28,598) with very few failures overall.

The SRA suitability factors are designed to exclude an individual who:

- is under indictment for a crime punishable by imprisonment for a term exceeding 1 year

- was convicted in any court of a crime punishable by imprisonment for a term exceeding 1 year

---

10. The Patriot Act also covers all entities (except for federal, state, or local governmental agencies), the responsible official (RO), the alternate RO, and each individual who owns or controls a private entity (academic, non-profit, commercial, or other). This chapter will only discuss the SRA as it pertains to individuals.

11. The RO, alternate RO, and individuals who own or control a private entity undergo a renewal SRA every three years.

- is a fugitive from justice

- is an unlawful user of any controlled substance

- is an alien illegally or unlawfully in the United States

- has been adjudicated as mentally impaired or has been committed to any mental institution

- is an alien who is a national of a country as to which the Secretary of State has made a determination (that remains in effect) that such country has repeatedly provided support for acts of international terrorism

- has been discharged from the Armed Services of the United States under dishonorable conditions

The SRA notably does not consider suitability determinations for financial status, organizational associations, nor does it require initial/random drug testing. In addition, and unlike suitability determinations for access to classified national security information or even work in the Nuclear Personnel Reliability Program (NPRP), the SRA automatically excludes any individual who illegally used a controlled substance at any time in his or her past or was convicted of a felony charge.

In 2005, DoD instituted an additional program, the BPRP, that supplements the national program legislated by the Patriot Act. Table 8 summarizes the similarities and differences in the DoD BPRP, NPRP, and other government, academia, and industry BPRP and NPRP programs. Due to its relative immaturity, the BPRP is wrestling with some implementation issues, which include: drug testing; conflicting suitability attributes between Personnel Security Investigations (PSIs) for access to National Security classified information and BSAT work; reporting mechanisms; locally administered interviews; proper level of personnel security investigations; and associations, especially with animal rights   activities.

Table 8. A Comparison of NPRP and BPRP

	DoD		Other BPRP			Other NPRP
	BPRP	**NPRP**	**GOVERNMENT**	**ACADEMIA**	**INDUSTRY**	**DoE**
Foreign Nationals	YES[a]	NO	YES	YES	NO[b]	NO
National Security Clearances	SMALL[b]	100%	SMALL	NO	MIXED[c]	100%
Use of National Security Investigations	YES	YES	YES	NO	MIXED	YES
Additional Investigations (USA Patriot Act Requirement: DOJ Select Agent)	YES	NO	YES	YES	YES	
Polygraphs	NO	LIMITED	NO	NO	NO	YES
Waivers:						
Felony Convictions	NO	YES	NO	NO	NO	YES
Illegal Drug Usage	NO	YES	NO	NO	NO	YES
Safety Suitability	NO	NO	YES	NO	NO	YES
Medical Screening	YES	YES	YES	YES	YES	YES
Random Urinalysis	MIXED[c]	100%	NO	MIXED	NA[d]	YES
Certifying Official Review Investigation Information	NO	YES	YES	NA	NA	YES
Failure Rate	<.1%	~1.8% in 2007	NA	NA	NA	NA
Size/Duration	2004	1960s	2004	2004	2004	1960s

a. DoD overseas labs are manned with foreign nationals.

b. Naval Surface Warfare Center—Dahlgren Division (NSWCDD) requires a secret clearance to work on the base. Therefore, everyone working with BSATs at NSWCDD Chemical, Biological ,and Radiological Defense Division possesses at least a secret clearance. One industry lab reported few national security clearances and one lab reported 100% clearances. The lab with 100% clearances had extensive experience with nuclear personnel reliability programs (PRP).

c. Urinalysis is performed under national security clearance vice BPRP.

d. Data not available.

Note: DOE Human Reliability Program law: http://ecfr.gpoaccess.gov/cgi/t/text/text-idx?c=ecfr&tpl=/ecfrbrowse/Title10/10cfr712_main_02.tpl.

Drug testing of military personnel is accomplished throughout the entire DoD. Therefore, drug testing for military personnel working on BSAT is easily accomplished. However, performance of comprehensive drug testing is difficult for non-military individuals. Most civil service positions do not contain a provision for drug testing in the position description. Therefore, civilians working on BSAT cannot routinely undergo drug testing. Other government agencies reported the same problem to the task force.

In some instances, civilian BSAT workers receive security clearances. A condition for obtaining a security clearance is subjecting oneself to drug testing. Therefore, any individual with a security clearance who is also in the BPRP can undergo drug screening. The number of BSAT workers with security clearances varies by command, *i.e.*, some of the larger commands having a low percentage of BSAT workers possessing security clearances whereas the smaller commands possessing a large percentage of individuals with security clearances. Therefore, the percentage of civilians who undergo drug testing varies by command. Some commands issued waivers to exclude civilian workers from drug testing while other commands' civilian workers voluntarily underwent drug testing. These purposeful activities would not be required if a change was made to the civilian position descriptions that included drug testing.

Contractor personnel also did not face mandatory drug testing unless the contract specifically called for drug testing. The government was in the process of renegotiating these contracts to include drug testing while the task force was conducting its work.

The task force heard several discussions regarding the proper PSI required for BPRP individuals (The different types of PSIs are outlined in Appendix B. Some government officials suggested that every individual working on BSAT should receive the most rigorous type of investigation (Single Scope Background Investigation (SSBI)) due to a belief that the SSBI investigation substantially increased prediction of unsuitable individuals. Other government officials, especially those outside DoD, worried that such a requirement would increase costs and insert time delays before individuals could perform work without providing any substantial benefit to the overall program reliability. The lowest investigation costs approximately $100 and the most expensive investigation costs $3,500.

The task force received statistics from DoD's NPRP that suggested the use of SSBIs may not substantially increase the accuracy of individual suitability. The overall failure rate for all individuals in the NPRP was 1.83 percent (310/16498); critical accounted for 0.8 percent (140/16498), whereas non-critical was 1.03 percent (170/16498). This one-year snapshot of a more mature and larger program suggested that an examination of the use of the PSI system to conduct personnel suitability checks needs to be evaluated. All NPRP critical positions receive SSBIs, yet the decertification rate is approximately the same, irrespective of investigation type.

In contrast to the proposal to make all BPRP individuals undergo an SSBI, the DoD nuclear PRP segments its workforce into two categories: critical and non-critical. A critical position is someone who possesses both technical knowledge and access to the nuclear weapon/system (*e.g.*, launch officers, maintenance personnel, etc.), and non-critical is an individual who possesses access but not technical knowledge (*e.g.*, guard forces). The NPRP designates the type of background investigation based upon the critical/non-critical position designation. Military personnel may also have the background investigation dictated by a need to access higher levels of classified material. In the case where different types of background investigations are called for, the more restrictive will always be conducted. One non-DoD organization (NIH) is already moving to a critical/non-critical designation of BPRP.

The PSIs can be used for military, civil service, and contractor personnel. However, they face severe constraints in their applicability to foreign nationals working in their host country. Investigation types are negotiated on a country-by-country basis and are subject to host nation requirements and capabilities. This issue has little to no bearing on U.S.-based labs, but does significantly impact overseas labs, which serve an important role in the nation's biodefense and global emerging infections surveillance program.

Use of PSIs allows the certifying official to conduct financial checks that should identify bankruptcy or other financial patterns that support the task force's concern about plausible blackmail scenarios. Although PSIs as currently constructed are fairly comprehensive, the questions regarding associations are designed to detect treasonous efforts or association with groups working to overthrow the federal government. The standard questions posed in a PSI do not appear to address any membership or support in animal rights groups. Since animal testing is the only mechanism to test prophylactic efficacy, any association with an animal rights group should be questioned.

The final issue uncovered by the task force involving the use of the PSI to inform the BPRP certifying official concerned access to the investigation results. Normally the actual investigation results are not provided to the local command. Results are passed to adjudicators, who examine all factors and then make a determination if the individual is eligible for some level of clearance. The clearance eligibility is then passed to the local command. DoD is evolving to an electronic-based system, termed Joint Personnel Adjudication System (JPAS), that indicates the person is eligible for a clearance. The local command can then authorize access to the appropriate level of clearance required by the command.

In some DoD commands, the certifying official used the eligibility determination as the basis to certify suitability for BPRP. However, adjudicators for national security clearance decisions can provide waivers for some of the areas specifically prohibited by the Patriot Act. Waiver decisions are not normally indicated or shared in eligibility decisions. Therefore, the official would not know that the individual may be a convicted felon or former drug user whose past transgressions were one time issues and have since demonstrated sufficiently good behavior to be deemed low risk for access to national security information. The NPRP and other programs with more stringent suitability requirements recognize this and require the certifying official to review the investigation results before making a determination.

In the case of the DoD NPRP, the certifying official is given sufficient latitude to make a favorable suitability determination if the facts of the case warrant it. However, they may also judge the case differently, resulting in an individual that may have access to the highest levels of classified information but not allowed to fill a critical nuclear position. The task force recommends that the BPRP certifying official review the results of each investigation to ensure they do not violate the Patriot Act suitability determinations. The task force did not find out which databases are checked by the SRA compared to each type of PSI, so it could not be certain that the different investigations would uncover the same information.

In addition to the issues identified above, the task force became aware of a government-wide effort aimed at increasing the speed of the PSI process. The Security and Suitability Process Reform report (December 2008) can be accessed via the web.[12] The implications for BPRP or other reliability programs were not

---

12. (Accessed May 11, 2009)
http://georgewbush-whitehouse.archives.gov/omb/reports/joint_security_dec2008.pdf

fully fleshed out for the task force upon completion of its work but the report promises a substantial revision and improvement on all PRP processes. The revamped investigation process promises much faster and, perhaps, tailored suitability determinations that could conceivably be conducted on demand, perhaps prior to entry into a BSAT containment suite. Such on-demand checks are comparable to certain industry sector checks that the task force did not have time to investigate (*e.g.*, gaming industry, aircraft crew checks). Senior officials should recognize that an overly restrictive PSI process can be as dangerous to the nation's biodefense effort by rejecting qualified and dedicated candidates who would make a positive contribution to the nation's biodefense efforts, as well as rejecting nefarious individuals.

In addition to the background checks conducted as part of the PSI process, the PRP certifying official conducts an interview of each individual in the BPRP as the final step in the certification process. The task force identified two areas requiring further evaluation. The number of certifying officials differed significantly between commands. This was due to a conflict to minimize the number of officials in some commands to ensure a consistent application of the BPRP, versus a desire to have the certifying official as close and familiar with each individual under the official's cognizance (necessitating a large number of certifying officials). The task force did not evaluate the effectiveness of either approach but suggests this is an area requiring further assessment.

The task force also received information regarding the use of local assessments to determine safety and psychological states of the BPRP individuals. These assessments by one non-DoD government agency appeared to be another mechanism to assist the certifying official in the performance of their duties. The assessments were based on standardized questionnaires that supposedly had some objective and scientific basis to determine the respondent's psychological profile and attitude towards safety. Although the task force did not have the time to assess the efficacy of the questionnaires, they were favorably inclined towards at least the safety questionnaire since this attempt was the first effort by any organization to determine the individual's attitude towards laboratory safety. If the safety assessment efficacy could demonstrably improve laboratory safety, then this would be a good practice to incorporate in the DoD BPRP.

Finally, the task force was not made aware of any reporting requirements to notify any centralized location of an individual's permanent removal from the BPRP or the BSAT certification process. The task force is concerned that an individual could conceivably be removed from one command's BPRP, move to another BSAT facility (either internal or external to DoD) and commence work on BSAT material.

There will always be potential instability or other threats that remain undetected and undeterred (*e.g.*, blackmail or financial stress), so one question is how far to push intrusiveness and at what cost. Common wisdom is that as emotional monitoring increases in intrusion, the best researchers will leave DoD laboratories for similar but higher paying positions in academia and industry. A counter-example is NSA, which has large numbers of excellent mathematicians, extremely intrusive monitoring of mental and emotional health, and an extremely effective employee assistance program. The NPRP is another extremely intrusive program that is widely accepted; it has a 50-year history without stigma over temporary disqualifications.

There are currently no reliable psychological tests for mental and emotional health, with polygraphs being the best example; a recent study by the National Academy of Sciences, indicates that polygraphs are not reliable.[13] NIH uses a series of four tests to evaluate psychological stability, substance abuse, and safety attitudes, but their utility ultimately depends on the truthfulness of the individual.

The task force considered several options for improving the BPRP and detection of potential security problems, including the following:

1. More frequent interviews and background checks. This could make effective use of the automated records check currently being installed in DoD.

2. Much longer retention of video records than the current 30–45 days commonly used in many labs, and much better exploitation of their potential value.

3. Management spot review of the video on a regular basis. This could and should be focused on safety, with security as a byproduct. A senior manager should periodically go over random samples of each investigator's records monthly and meet with the individuals to discuss the safety practices.

---

13. National Research Council (2003). *The Polygraph and Lie Detection*. Committee to Review the Scientific Evidence on the Polygraph. Division of Behavioral and Social Sciences and Education. Washington, D.C.: The National Academies Press.

4. Clearer management accountability and training in monitoring researchers and labs in their daily behavior.

5. Self-assessment forms modified to require a signature of the individual and with a printed clause of the legal penalties for false information.

6. Monitor the individual laboratory support systems (*e.g.*, specialized Supervisory Control and Data Acquisition (SCADA)) to look for deviations from the norm.

7. Intrusive monitor of emotional state, such as <u>effective</u> polygraphs (if and when they exist), or reviewing off-site medical records.

8. Two-person rule in labs.

In order to provide structure to the relative evaluation of these options, the task force judged each in terms of the following two criteria: (1) incremental improvement in detection and deterrence of malfeasance (performance), and (2) cost of added intrusion in terms of mission-effectiveness, quality of staff, dollars, etc.

Safety and security are affected differently by most of these criteria and the metrics are clearly subjective. The results of the evaluation are shown in Figure 3. The conclusions drawn from this collective judgment is that options 1–5 are most effective while 6–8 are rated as more costly and less effective.

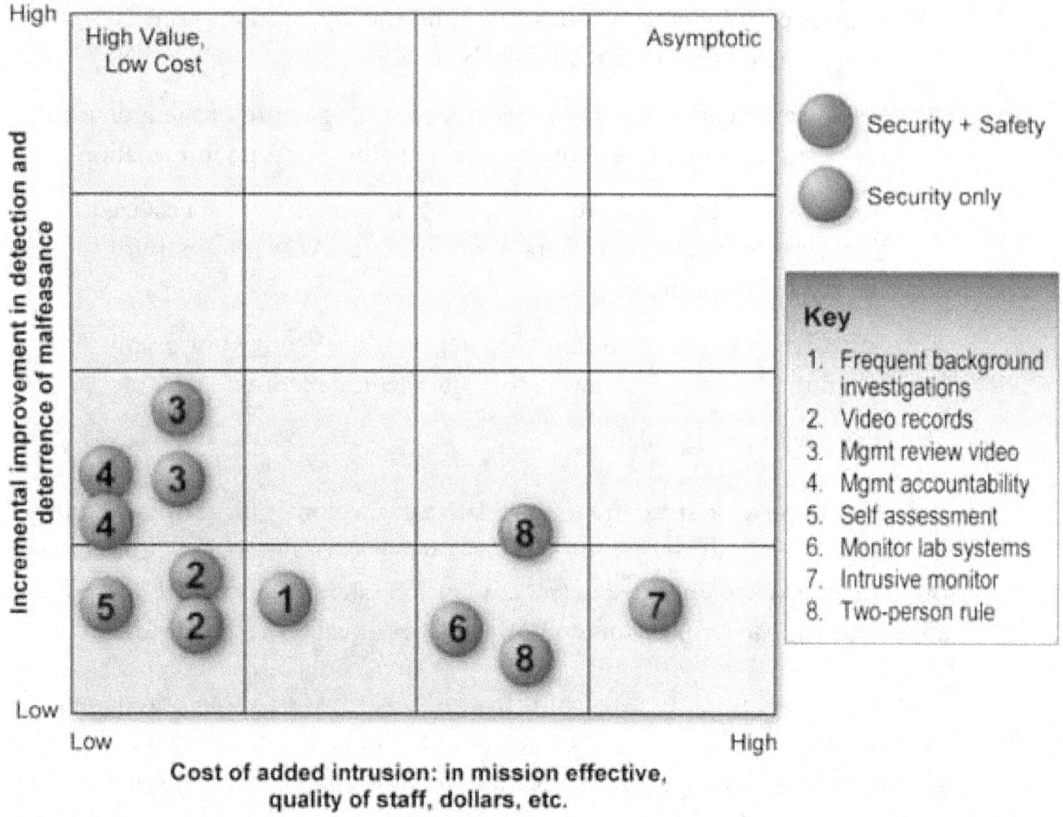

Figure 3. Subjectively Considered Improvements in Security as Compared to Cost

BPRP Findings

- The PSI process can and does include checks on financial status, alcohol dependency, and organization associations. However, there does not appear to be any mechanism to determine association with an animal rights organization.

- The PSI process does not apply to foreign nationals working overseas.

- Drug testing of BPRP personnel is inconsistent and cannot be conducted routinely on civilian (civil service and contractor) personnel.

- The efficacy of an SSBI for a worker in the BPRP is not clear.

- Not all BPRP COs request the actual results of BPRP-nominated individuals.

- Two different and contradictory ideas exist regarding the number of COs for a given command size.

- The efficacy of local behavioral and safety attitude checks varies among different BPRP organizations.

- The impact of the recent multi-agency task force on Security and Suitability Process Reform on the DoD BPRP is unknown.

- There is no known requirement to report an individual permanently removed from a local command's BPRP to a central organization or the BSAT certifying authority.

Chapter 5. Findings and Recommendations

Overarching Finding

> A determined adversary cannot be prevented from obtaining very dangerous biological materials intended for nefarious purposes, if not from DoD labs, then from other sources. The best we can do is to make it more difficult. We need to recognize this reality and be prepared to mitigate the effects of a biological attack. We, as a nation, are not prepared.

General Findings

- The task force found that in the DoD facilities they assessed, the safety and security programs are as good as or better than in comparably sized facilities in other government, industry, and academic sectors.
  - DoD regulations exceed those imposed by CDC.
  - This finding is based on briefings, interviews, and observations but without any direct means to observe actual practices.
  - Several of the new non-DoD BSL labs are more modern and, if USAMRIID is to stay in the forefront and address evolving threats, investment in new infrastructure must be sufficient.
- A strong safety record of the laboratories is a good indicator of the general effectiveness of safety measures.
- Safety and security require substantial investment. Research programs cannot bear this cost.
- The "isolated" computer system could represent a serious vulnerability but the task force did not have the resources to verify this.
- The insider threat dominates internal security concerns.

- An insider could probably transfer BSAT out of the facility or supply chain without discovery, regardless of defensive countermeasures. One can only make it difficult and uncertain for the insider.

- Detection of an insider threat is difficult even with extensive monitoring of the emotional and mental state of BSAT-certified employees, including transport personnel.

- Improved video monitoring of labs can be superior to the two-person rule for detecting or deterring nefarious activities in the lab, and can be valuable in assuring good safety practices.

- BSAT transport works well today using the "lost in the crowd" approach (very large numbers moved every day), and may be worse with a two-person rule.

- Inspections are needed, but are currently burdensome (too many, different guidelines, lack of expertise, etc.) and should be improved.

- Advancing technology is increasing ease of terrorist access to BSAT worldwide making it urgent to support the long-term development of broad-spectrum diagnostics, therapeutics, vaccines, and consequence management capabilities.

- Rather than steal BSAT from a DoD lab, other paths would appear preferable for an adversary (*e.g.*, natural sources, non-DoD labs, non-U.S. labs, genomic synthesis), except possibly in the case of a blackmailed or disgruntled employee working from the inside.

- DoD should avoid those measures that are significantly detrimental to the laboratory mission, that are onerous, or that detract from morale unless the measure significantly improves security or safety.

- Covert external threats are unlikely and layers of defensive measures serve to further deter.

- An external "attack" by a demonstration mob or explosives, coupled with inflammatory media, could panic the surrounding populace.

- Public education now is the best way to mitigate public panic later, if there is a loss or perceived loss of containment.

Recommendations

RECOMMENDATION #1. CYBER RED TEAM

Conduct red team reviews of the computer systems at USAMRIID (and, depending on results, other DoD labs):

- Independent red team review of the "isolated computer systems" for actual loss of isolation, both current and possible.

- This review should be thorough and conducted by a team with deep cyber experience (*e.g.*, NSA or Army Net Ops).

- Instruct that team to identify actual or potential access to these "isolated computers" via added connections, malicious hardware or software (there is extensive wiring throughout the buildings), radio frequency leakage, and other measures. There may be wireless connections; however, the task force was not able to verify one way or the other. Connections to one or more of the external nets (*e.g.*, NIPRNET) could open the door to external manipulation.

- The insider threat and SCADA vulnerability should dominate this focus (two non-DoD labs had either wireless or remote wired access).

A different team familiar with lab functionality should determine what actions a malefactor might be able to do with such connections and develop a plan for mitigating this risk.

The two recommended actions together will identify and evaluate the vulnerabilities and provide the basis for the decisions to make improvements in the computer systems at DoD labs: (1) a review by an independent and extremely competent information assurance team to evaluate the presumed "isolation" of the computer systems, including ways in which a malefactor might subvert the systems; and (2) a study by a team familiar with the practices, layout, and equipment to assess what harm could be done by knowledgeable malefactors with full access to the computer systems.

RECOMMENDATION #2. MONITORING ACTIVITIES

Make minor changes in the procedures used to monitor activities in labs to improve effectiveness without introducing significantly obtrusive measures that are unwarranted by the threat:

- Retain video records of lab surveillance for a minimum of 1 year and a random 5 percent of records for 5 years.

- Assign management accountability and provide training for monitoring of researchers in daily lab work.

- Managers and supervisors sample video records of each lab worker on no less than a monthly basis and provide mandatory feedback to each worker on safety practices. Develop tools for this review that make it easier and more effective (*e.g.*, record only when lab is occupied, metadata, user friendly editing and search, etc.).

- Discourage attempts to impose a two-person rule for security as being counter-productive in most situations.

- Hold an annual meeting of all BPRP personnel to remind them of values, moral obligations, and observations that ought to be reported.

The recommended actions are taken from those judged to contribute to better performance and lower cost. Primary among these is more direct management responsibility and more effective use of video recordings. The greatest cost of all task force recommendations is the implicit upgrading of the video system to provide full coverage and extended retention of the video data.

RECOMMENDATION #3. BIOLOGICAL PERSONNEL RELIABILITY PROGRAM

Maintain use of BPRP tailored to bio-defense work; balance risk from a malevolent insider against detriment to laboratory mission:

- Develop consistent suitability attributes for biodefense work, *e.g.*, no affiliation with animal rights activists.

- Automate suitability checks (no less than annual but transition to monthly/weekly/daily periodicity using Automated Record Checks).

- Provide training to produce effective certifying officials and certifying medical authorities.

- Review of dossiers from background investigations by certifying officials.

- Establish clear management accountability and training in monitoring researchers in their daily behavior.

- Assess safety attitude explicitly.[14]

- Include penalty statement for providing false information in the "self assessment" forms that include questions related to emotional and mental state; have employees sign the form. This form could be used by all DoD labs working with BSATs.

- Create a database of persons permanently removed from BPRP in cooperation with HHS/USDA and make this accessible by human resources personnel in appropriate organizations.

The improvements in the BPRP, aside from the specific actions listed, focus on more direct management involvement and encouraging a safety attitude across the work force. The recommended actions are drawn from the options that provide significant improvement with the least intrusiveness.

---

14. NIH does this with a safety questionnaire.

RECOMMENDATION #4: OCONUS LABORATORIES

Issue blanket waiver to use Department of State background investigations (conducted by U.S. Embassy Regional Security Office) in place of the National Agency Check with Local Agency Check and Credit (NACLC) among local national personnel working with BSAT in OCONUS labs.

- OCONUS laboratories can comply with all BPRP regulations except the NACLC Personnel Security Investigation, which cannot be performed OCONUS.

Grant waiver authority to laboratory commanders to determine minimum security measures for shipments based on local risk assessment and conditions for which shipment must occur (*e.g.*, public health, forensic analysis).

- CONUS transportation rules limit the timely detection and/or diagnosis of highly pathogenic organisms, such as avian influenza, and may preclude treatment and development of vaccines.

- Transportation should occur under the most secure alternative available and should ensure active monitoring and immediate notification of delivery.

This recommendation calls for recognition that OCONUS labs operate in a different environment than those in CONUS. The primary responsibilities of OCONUS labs are to develop effective medical countermeasures for protection against naturally occurring infectious diseases in their endemic regions and for surveillance of naturally occurring pathogens such as the avian influenza. These labs are co-located with labs of the host nation.

RECOMMENDATION #5: COMPLIANCE INSPECTIONS

Provide resources for an independent inspection team comprising authoritative and successful individuals:

- Team member should have expertise gained by successful completion of inspected position (not just by course completion).

- Establish training programs for inspectors to promote expertise.

- Inspect both worker practices and management ability to effectively monitor worker practices (use video tape sampling to observe safety practices).

- Report common deficiencies to the user community.

- Function only as an inspection team, not mentors or trainers.

- Conduct sufficient number of inspections to maintain expertise:

  - Joint DoD inspection team or CDC participation.

Engage other organizations concerned with bio safety and security to:

- Develop consistency among compliance inspection programs. Define common inspection standards and criteria.

- Establish a coordination initiative to share inspection results that could reduce multiple inspections.

- Work towards one team satisfying the needs of multiple organizations.

Compliance inspections are an important element of both bio-safety and bio-security. Currently, parent organizations field teams of varying qualifications and abilities. Ideally, there should be one very competent team that inspects all such labs and therefore conducts inspections often enough to assure their own currency and competence, and does so against a common set of regulations and policies. This recommendation would place DoD on a track to create one joint team, the conceptual basis for an eventual national inspection team for BSATs.

RECOMMENDATION #6: BSAT TRANSPORTATION

- Review use of two-person rule for BSAT shipments:

  - Threat is unlikely.

  - Escort would tend to draw attention to the shipment.

  - Theft would require knowledge of shipping information, potentially by penetration of computer systems or by insider.

  - Recognize that a terrorist interception could use force and kill or capture the driver, escort, etc., in some relatively remote truck stop.

- This rule would likely force the rest of the bio-defense community to follow suit and that would be extremely expensive.

- Continue to use "lost in the crowd" approach used by all, for the shipments involving DoD labs.

- As a future option, investigate potential of tamper-resistant shipment containers (Defense Threat Reduction Agency (DTRA) technology)

  - Design and develop tamper resistant shipment containers that look like any other bio-hazard shipment but which destroys the samples if accessed without the proper controls and which is acceptable for public transport.

There are rational arguments against the two-person rule for transport of BSAT materials and it could well be that it would create lessened security. The current practice of shipping with bio-hazard labels and utilizing UPS or FedEx, adopts a "lost in the crowd" approach. In addition, the threat is unlikely unless the malefactor has very specific information from either an insider or penetration of the lab computers. In the future, this threat and circumstances may be of greater concern, in which case further action may be advisable. The arms control community has developed tamper-resistant containers and that technology should be extended to accommodate pathogen shipments should the need arise.

RECOMMENDATION #7: PUBLIC EDUCATION AND RELATIONS

- Educate the public in the regions near the labs on mission, safety measures and level of risk, to counter an attack intended to inflame the media and close the facility.

- All CONUS bio-containment facilities and their immediate senior commands within DoD should develop a risk communication plan and a public relations plan, with a media portion to respond to any emergency response:

  - that entail loss of BSAT, or

  - issues that could be perceived by the media as an endangerment to public health or community relations.

Planning before there is a problem is always preferred to *ad hoc* reactions during an event. In addition, early public education is the best way to mitigate potential public panic in the future, if there is an actual or perceived loss of containment.

Chapter 6. Summary and Closing Remarks

The task force has offered recommendations in the following seven areas:

- cyber red team

- monitoring activities in the labs

- enhancing the Biological Personnel Reliability Program

- OCONUS regulations

- compliance inspections

- BSAT transport

- public education and relations

There is a modest dollar cost to implement these recommendations that the task force believes should not be paid out of research funding. There is little intangible cost (*e.g.*, interference with mission, morale).

The task force, by its charter focused on DoD labs and concluded that DoD labs are equally or better protected than non-DoD labs. However, it also concluded that a determined adversary could obtain dangerous BSAT from a number of sources outside DoD. The planning assumption should be that the country may have to endure a biological attack sometime in the future and that DoD should be more active in the interagency arena to assure a realistic balance between prevention and consequence management.

Appendix A. BSL Laboratories Included in Study

This appendix contains brief descriptions of BSL laboratories included in this study. The task force either conducted site visits, or received briefings from each of these facilities.

The United States Army Medical Research Institute for Infectious Diseases (USAMRIID)

USAMRIID conducts basic and applied research on biological threats resulting in medical solutions to protect military service members. USAMRIID, an organization of the U.S. Army Medical Research and Materiel Command, is the lead medical research laboratory for the U.S. Biological Defense Research Program. The Institute plays a key role as the only DoD laboratory equipped to safely study highly hazardous infectious agents requiring maximum containment at biosafety level 4. As the center of excellence for DoD medical biological defense research, USAMRIID's challenge is to maintain its world-class scientific and technology base while being responsive to its primary customer—the warfighter.

Walter Reed Army Institute of Research (WRAIR)

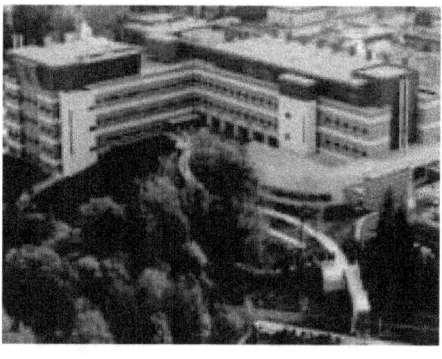

WRAIR's mission is to conduct biomedical research that is responsive to DoD and U.S. Army requirements and deliver life-saving products, including knowledge, technology, and medical materiel that sustain the combat effectiveness of the warfighter. WRAIR's focus on research for the soldiers affects all aspects of its operations because military medical research priorities differ from those of the civilian sector.

WRAIR scientists have a unique understanding of military operations and environments, including the stresses and exposures troops encounter and the performance requirements of a deployed military force. Despite WRAIR's focus on the military, its research has been used to solve nonmilitary medical problems around the world.

Naval Medical Research Center (NMRC)

NMRC is focused on finding solutions to both traditional battlefield medical problems, such as bleeding, traumatic brain injury, combat stress, and naturally occurring infectious diseases, as well as health problems associated with non-conventional weapons, including thermobaric blast, biological agents, and radiation. The laboratories play a  highly critical role in the worldwide monitoring of emerging infectious diseases, including avian influenza and others of the future that threaten both deployed forces and world civilizations. They also support theater security cooperation through international military-to-military collaborations and public health capacity-building efforts, and by responding to such disasters as the 2004 tsunami in Banda Aceh, Indonesia and the more recent earthquakes in central Java and Peru.

Edgewood Chemical Biological Center (ECBC)

ECBC's science and technology expertise has protected the United States from the threat of chemical weapons since 1917. Since that time, the Center has expanded its mission to include biological materials and emerges today as the nation's premier authority on chemical and biological defense. ECBC activities  span the life cycle of chemical and biological defense research and product development. An organizational grandchild of the original Edgewood Arsenal, ECBC has provided chemical and biological solutions to the warfighter for nearly a century.

United States Army Medical Research Institute of Chemical Defense (USAMRICD)

USAMRICD is the nation's leading science and technology laboratory in the area of medical chemical countermeasures research and development. With sophisticated laboratories located at Aberdeen Proving Ground, Maryland, USAMRICD manages a diversified portfolio of medical chemical warfare agent research projects for the Department of Defense and other Federal Agencies. Its mission is to discover and develop medical countermeasures to chemical warfare agents for U.S. military and U.S. citizens, to train and educate personnel in the medical management of chemical casualties, and to provide subject matter expertise in developing Defense and National policy and in proper crisis management.

Dahlgren Naval Surface Warfare Center (DNSWC)

DNSWC provides research, development, test and evaluation, analysis, systems engineering, integration, and certification of complex naval warfare systems related to surface warfare, strategic systems, combat and weapons systems associated with surface warfare. It provides system integration and certification for weapons, combat systems, and warfare systems, and executes other responsibilities as assigned by the Commander, Naval Surface Warfare Center.

West Desert Test Center (WDTC)

The Life Sciences Division's mission is to design, perform, and report results of biological defense testing in support of the WDTC mission: to safely test our warfighters' future equipment to the highest standards within cost and schedule. Testing is performed in the field with biosimulant aerosol challenge materials. In BSL-2 and -3 laboratories, respectively, biological simulants and select agents are aerosolized to test detection, decontamination, and protection systems. Additionally, the division provides materials and a staff of scientists as expert support for testing at Dugway Proving Ground, as well as biological defense worldwide.

711th Human Performance Wing (HPW)

The 711th HPW is the first human-centric warfare wing to consolidate research, consultation, and education under one roof. The 711th HPW merges the Air Force Research Laboratory Human Effectiveness Directorate with the 311th Human Systems Wing, currently located at Brooks Air Force Base, the Performance Enhancement Directorate, and the U.S. Air Force School of Aerospace Medicine, which recently integrated the Air Force Institute for Operational Health. The wing's primary mission areas are aerospace medicine, science and technology, and human systems integration.

Armed Forces Institute of Pathology (AFIP)

The Armed Forces Institute of Pathology focuses on innovative scientific research in fields such as environmental pathology and toxicology, infectious diseases, oncology, and forensic science.

Centers for Disease Control and Prevention (CDC)

The CDC regulates the possession, use, and transfer of select agents and toxins that have the potential to pose a severe threat to public health and safety. The CDC Select Agent Program oversees these activities and registers all laboratories and other entities in the United States that possess, use, or transfer a select agent or toxin.

National Biodefense Analysis and Countermeasures Center (NBACC)

The NBACC provides the nation with essential biocontainment laboratory space for biological threat characterization and bioforensic research. The NBACC facility, managed by Department of Homeland Security's Science & Technology directorate in accordance with the Homeland Security Act of 2002 and the Homeland Security Presidential Directive entitled "Biodefense for the 21st Century," is located within the National Interagency Biodefense Campus at Fort Detrick, Maryland.

National Institute of Allergy and Infectious Diseases (NIAID)

The NIAID conducts and supports basic and applied research to better understand, treat, and ultimately prevent infectious, immunologic, and allergic diseases. NIAID offices and laboratories are located in Bethesda, Maryland near the NIH main campus and in Hamilton, Montana.

Viral Immunology Center (VIC), Georgia State University

The VIC consists of four components centered on the needs and research interests of Georgia Research Alliance Eminent Scholar Dr. Julia Hilliard: the BSL-3/BSL-4 glove-box facility, the clinical diagnostic test laboratory, research and development laboratories, and the business office.

National Emerging Infectious Diseases Laboratories (NEIDL), Boston University

The NEIDL is part of a national network of secure facilities that study infectious diseases, whether they occur naturally or are introduced deliberately through bioterrorism. The facility is dedicated to the development of diagnostics, vaccines, and therapeutics to combat emerging and re-emerging infectious diseases. In addition to BSL-2 and BSL-3 laboratories, the NEIDL will house a BSL-4 laboratory that operates at the highest level of containment. The NEIDL will add to the growing life sciences industry in the region, throughout the Commonwealth of Massachusetts, and across the country.

Battelle Biomedical Research Center West Jefferson Biomedical Facility (BBBRC)

The BBBRC is one of the largest private biomedical laboratories in the country. Researchers and scientists perform vital work, including testing new vaccines, therapeutics, and antidotes supporting a variety of government biological defense programs and pharmaceutical company product development. Research conducted

at the West Jefferson complex also has contributed to medical advances in emerging infectious diseases, medical chemical defense therapeutics, and treatment for infant botulism. The center has conducted research for the last 23 years into protective measures against chemical and biological threats faced by U.S. troops.

Midwest Research Institute (MRI)

MRI is an independent, not-for-profit, contract research organization. To address the growing demand for expertise in laboratory services, the MRI Center for Biological Safety and Security is staffed by an internationally recognized team of certified bio-safety and security specialists dedicated to providing a diverse range of specialized laboratory consulting services, from design, to operations, to management.

Southwest Foundation for Biomedical Research (SFBR)

SFBR is one of the world's leading independent biomedical research institutions, SFBR is dedicated to advancing the health of our global community through innovative biomedical research. Located on a 332-acre campus on the northwest side of San Antonio, Texas, SFBR partners with hundreds of researchers and institutions around the world, targeting advances in the fight against cardiovascular disease, diabetes, obesity, cancer, psychiatric disorders, problems of pregnancy, AIDS, hepatitis, malaria, parasitic infections, and a host of other infectious diseases. It has a staff of more than 400 employees.

The University of Texas – Medical Branch (UTMB)

UTMB was established in 1891 as the University of Texas Medical Department, UTMB has grown from one building, 23 students and 13 faculty members to a modern health science center with more than 70 major buildings, more than 2,500 students, and more than 1,000 faculty. The 84-acre campus includes four schools, three institutes for advanced study, a major medical library, a network of hospitals and clinics that provide a full range of primary and specialized medical care, an affiliated Shriners Burns Hospital, and numerous research facilities. UTMB is a component of the University of Texas System. The mission of The University of Texas – Medical Branch at Galveston is to provide scholarly teaching, innovative scientific investigation, and state-of-the-art patient care in a learning environment to better the health of society.

Naval Medical Research Center Detachment (NMRCD)

NMRCD conducts research on and surveillance of a wide range of infectious diseases that threaten military operations in the region. NMRCD partners with the Peruvian Army and Navy and works closely with prestigious universities like Cayetano-Heredia and San Marcos. Since its inception in 1983, NMRCD has capitalized on its access to infectious disease threats endemic to South America through strong institutional partnerships. The disease surveillance programs engage more than two dozen institutions in ten South American nations. Using its permanent field laboratory and staff at Iquitos on the Amazon River in eastern Peru, NMRCD worked with numerous collaborators to document the spread of dengue fever and its vectors through the Amazon River basin.

Naval Medical Research Unit Three (NAMRU-3)

The mission of NAMRU-3, based in Cairo, Egypt, is to conduct infectious disease research and to carry out public health activities, principally aimed toward improved disease surveillance and outbreak response assistance. Their command plays a key role in enhancing the health, safety, and readiness of DoD personnel assigned to Africa, the Middle East, and Southwest Asia in both peacetime and contingency missions. NAMRU-3 is the only research institution in North Africa with an Association for Assessment and Accreditation of Laboratory Animal Care International-accredited animal facility and is one of only two institutions in Africa with a BSL-3 laboratory. NAMRU-3 is playing an important role in the global response to the threat of avian influenza and pandemic influenza and is currently active in monitoring infectious disease trends among DoD personnel deployed to operational bases in Turkey, Afghanistan, and Iraq. Over the last 10 years, NAMRU-3 has conducted 69 disease outbreak investigations in 25 different countries.

U.S. Army Medical Component of the Armed Forces Research Institute of the Medical Sciences (USAMC-AFRIMS)

The Thai component of AFIRMS is a subordinate command within the Royal Thai Army Medical Department (RTAMD). The Director General, the organization's senior military officer, heads the collaboration. Within the Thai context, AFRIMS responds to the directed research needs of the RTAMD, which, among other things, includes the collaborative activities with U.S. counterparts focusing on infectious diseases of military and public health importance.

AFRIMS is the largest overseas U.S. Army biomedical research laboratory and plays a vital role in the study of tropical infectious diseases, conducting cutting-edge research and development projects that address the medical threats facing U.S. forces deployed in over 75 countries worldwide.

Rocky Mountain Laboratories (RML)

RML is a premier NIH facility for biomedical research. The lab is housed in a state-of-the-art facility in Hamilton, MT. A key component of the NIAID Division of Intramural Research, RML is perhaps best known for its research into vector-borne diseases. The scientific programs at RML are organized into five separate laboratories. Each laboratory  has a distinguished scientist as its Laboratory Chief, and a number of individual research groups that study specific infectious agents. In addition, RML's new Integrated Research Facility is the first NIH facility of its kind to house BSL-2, BSL-3, and BSL-4 laboratory space in one building along with administrative offices and conference rooms.

Appendix B. Types of Personnel Security Investigations

National Agency Check

The National Agency Check (NAC) consists of searches of the Security/Sustainability Investigation Index and the Defense Clearance and Investigations Index, as well as the FBI Identification Division's name and fingerprint files, and other files as necessary. These are conducted by the Office of Personnel Management.

National Agency Check and Inquiries

The National Agency Check and Inquiries (NACI) is a basic investigation required for all new federal employees. It consists of the National Agency Check investigation, as well as written inquires and record searches covering specific areas of a person's background during the past five years. Inquiries are sent to employers, schools attended, references given, and local law enforcement authorities.

NACI and Credit

The NACI and Credit (NACIC) consists of the NACI with the addition of a credit record check.

Access NACI

The Access NACI (ANACI) consists of a required initial investigation for federal employees who will need access to classified national security information at the Confidential and Secret levels. The ANACI includes the NACIC with additional local law enforcement agency checks.

NAC with Local Agency Check and Credit

The NAC with Local Agency Check and Credit (NACLC) is the initial investigation for government contractors at the Confidential and Secret national security access levels. The NACLC is also used to meet reinvestigation requirements for all individuals holding Confidential and Secret clearances.

Single Scope Background Investigation

The Single Scope Background Investigation (SSBI) is a government-wide investigation required for all personnel needing access to Top Secret classified national security information. The SSBI covers the last seven years of the person's activities and includes verification of citizenship and date and place of birth. In addition, the SSBI conducts national agency records checks on the person's spouse or cohabitant and interviews with selected references and former spouses.

SSBI–Periodic Reinvestigation

The SSBI–Periodic Reinvestigation (SSBI–PR) is required every five years for personnel with Top Secret security clearances.

Schedule

Investigations are nominally conducted on a five-year reinvestigation schedule. In some cases, a specific type of national security clearance may call for a reinvestigation on a faster schedule. Investigations for collateral Secret and lower clearances sometimes exceed five years due to budgeting or workload constraints.

Terms of Reference

OCT - 3 2008

MEMORANDUM FOR CHAIRMAN, DEFENSE SCIENCE BOARD

SUBJECT: Terms of Reference – Defense Science Board (DSB) Task Force on the
Department of Defense (DoD) Biological Safety and Security Program

DoD maintains the ability to develop defensive capability against select biological agents and toxins. DoD Directive 5210.88 and DoD Instruction 5210.89 establish minimum security standards for safeguarding biological select agents and toxins in the possession or custody of DoD against theft, loss, diversion, or unauthorized access or use, and that operations with such agents are conducted in a safe, secure, and reliable manner.

The study seeks to address the following major themes: Are current and proposed policies in DoD and Military Department's biological safety, security and biological personnel reliability programs adequate to safeguard against accidental or intentional loss/misuse of Biological Select Agents and Toxins (BSAT) by external or internal actors from the DoD and Military Department's RDT&E infrastructure? Are current DoD associated laboratories or operations that use or store BSAT meeting stringent standards for safety, security and personnel reliability? How do DoD and the Military Department's programs compare with other government agency programs, academic programs, and industry programs? How can DoD usefully employ experience in other areas requiring the utmost safety and reliability when handling dangerous material (e.g., the nuclear personnel reliability program) for biosurety policy development and implementation?

The study should survey operations in relevant U.S. academic and commercial sectors and may also draw on applicable information from other international biodefense programs. The study should identify barriers to an effective program and provide recommendations on actionable solutions for improvement.

The study will provide an interim report not later than December 1, 2008, of the program's comparative operation against current safety, security, and reliability standards. Follow-on tasking may be derived from the interim report.

The study will be sponsored by me as the Under Secretary of Defense for Acquisition, Technology and Logistics, the Secretary of the Army, and the Assistant to the Secretary of Defense for Nuclear and Chemical and Biological Defense Programs.

Mr. Larry Lynn will serve as the Task Force chairman. Colonel George Korch, USA, and Lieutenant Commander Franca R. Jones, USN, OASTD(NCB), will serve as Co-Executive Secretaries and Lieutenant Colonel Karen Walters, USA, will serve as the DSB Military Assistant.

The Task Force will operate in accordance with the provisions of P.L. 92-463, the "Federal Advisory Committee Act," and DoD Directive 5105.4, the "DoD Federal Advisory Committee Management Program." It is not anticipated that this Task Force will need to go into any "particular matters" within the meaning of title 18, United States Code, section 208, nor will it cause any member to be placed in the position of action as a procurement official.

John J. Young, Jr.

Study Participants

CHAIRMAN

Name	Affiliation
Mr. Larry Lynn	Private Consultant

EXECUTIVE SECRETARIES

LCDR Franca Jones	Assistant to the Secretary of Defense for Nuclear, Chemical, and Biological Defense Programs
COL George Korch	Office of the Deputy Chief of Staff of the Army G-3/5/7

MEMBERS

Dr. Emmett Barkley	Proven Practices, LLC
Dr. David Franz	Midwest Research Institute
Dr. Gigi Kwik Gronvall	University of Pittsburgh Medical Center
Dr. Steve Kornguth	University of Texas—Austin
Dr. Jonathon Richmond	Jonathan Richmond & Assoc., Inc.
Dr. Anna Skalka	Fox Chase Cancer Center

DSB REPRESENTATIVES

Mr. Brian Hughes	Executive Director—Defense Science Board
LTC Karen Walters	Defense Science Board

STAFF

Dr. Raj Gupta	Strategic Analysis, Inc.
Ms. Becky Bortnick	Strategic Analysis, Inc.
Ms. Kelly Frere	Strategic Analysis, Inc.
Mr. Gregory Byerly	Strategic Analysis, Inc.
Ms. Barbara Bicksler	Strategic Analysis, Inc.

Presentations and Task Force Site Visits

Name	Topic

OCTOBER 6, 2008

Site Visit to Southwest Biomedical Research Foundation	
Dr. Jean Patterson	Roundtable Discussion

OCTOBER 7, 2008

Site Visit to University of Texas—Austin	
Dr. Kenneth Shine, UT Chancellor	Discussion of UT–Medical Branch at Galveston, TX

OCTOBER 8, 2008

LTC Shoemaker and Dr. Patricia Worsham	Briefed Task Force at Kick-Off Meeting

OCTOBER 17, 2008

Site Visit to United States Medical Research Institute of Infectious Diseases (USAMRIID)	
COL John Skvorak, USAMRIID Commander	Roundtable Discussion
LTC David Shoemaker Director, Safety, Biosurety, Security	USAMRIID Security and Surety Program

OCTOBER 30, 2008

Site Visit to Centers for Disease Control and Prevention, Atlanta, GA	
Dr. Robbin Weyant, Director, CDC Division of Select Agents and Toxins	Introduction and Review of National Select Agent Requirements
Dr. Martin Sanders, Acting Director, CDC Office of Health and Safety	Review of Laboratory Safety Oversight
Dr. Anthony Sanchez, Manager, CDC Maximum Containment Laboratory	Management of CDC High Containment Research
Ms. Jacqueline Edwards, Chief, Personnel Security/Suitability Branch, CDC Office of Security and Emergency Preparedness	Personnel Security/Suitability Overview
Mr. James Pedone, Physical Security Operations Branch, CDC Office of Security and Emergency Preparedness	Physical Security Overview

OCTOBER 30, 2008

Site Visit to University of Georgia, Atlanta, GA	
Mr. Richard Muller, Jr. Bio Safety Officer	BSAT Programs at Georgia State University

OCTOBER 31, 2008

Site Visit to Walter Reed Army Institute of Research and Naval Medical Research Center	
CAPT John Christopher Daniel Commanding Officer	Naval Medical Research Center
COL Donald G Heppner Deputy Commander of WRAIR	Walter Reed Army Institute of Research
MAJ Amy King Joint Security Office	Safety Guidelines, Protocols, and Inspections
Ms. Tina Lovell Joint Bio Security Office /Responsible Official	Functions of the Office of Responsible Official
Mr. Bernard Pearce Physical Security Specialist	Physical Security Brief on External Building and Internal Laboratory Security Enhancements
Dr. Tom Geisbert Associate Director of NEIDL	Boston University Lab Overview
Dr. Thomas Moore Boston University Medical Center	Boston University Lab Overview

NOVEMBER 5, 2008

Mr. Todd Blose Army DAIG	Technical Inspections Division Overview
LTC Amy Korman Overseas Laboratory Operations Walter Reed Army Institute of Research	Walter Reed Army Institute of Research Special Foreign Activities
Dr. John Wade Battelle	Battelle's Perspective on Bio Security

NOVEMBER 6, 2008

CAPT (Ret.) Steve Walz, PhD Director, Field Laboratories Naval Medical Research Center	Navy OCONUS Labs; Overview and BSAT Issues
Mr. John Bunkall Personnel Reliability Program Manager, Chief Naval Operations	Biological Personnel Reliability Program for the Dept. of Navy
Mr. John Humpton, Army Personnel Reliability Program Manager	Fundamentals of the Army's Biological Personnel Reliability Program

NOVEMBER 12, 2008

Dr. Tom Sack Regional VP for Midwest Operations Midwest Research Institute (MRI)	Midwest Research Institute Select Agent Program
Mr. Mike Ehret Regional VP for Mid Atlantic Operations Midwest Research Institute (MRI)	Midwest Research Institute Select Agent Program
CDR Jeffrey Horton Office of the Deputy Assistant to the Secretary of Defense for Nuclear Matters	Nuclear Weapon Personnel Reliability Program (PRP)
Dr. Mike Callahan DARPA Program Manager	DARPA Program

NOVEMBER 17, 2008

Site Visit to National Institutes of Health, Bethesda, MD	
CAPT Deborah Wilson Director, Division of Occupational Health and Safety	National Institutes of Health (NIH) Biological Surety Program
Mr. Bill Cullen Associate Director for Security and Emergency Response, NIH	NIH Security
Dr. Katherine Zoon Director, Intramural Research, NIAID	NIH Intramural Research Programs
Dr. Rose M Hayden Safety Director, CBR Defense Division Laboratory, Dahlgren	Dahlgren NSWC BSAT Program
Ms. Meredith Bondurant CBR Defense Division Laboratory	Dahlgren NSWC BSAT Program

NOVEMBER 19, 2008

Site Visit to Edgewood Chemical Biological Center	
Coordinated by COL George Korch	Discussion with ECBC personnel

NOVEMBER 20, 2008

Dr. Douglas Andersen Chief, Life Sciences Division West Desert Test Center	Dugway Proving Grounds
COL Patricia Reilly Division Chief, Bio Sciences & Protection 711HPW/RHP	Task Force Review of the DoD Biological Surety Program and Bio Defense Research Portfolio

References and Regulations

References

National Research Council (2003). *The Polygraph and Lie Detection.* Committee to Review the Scientific Evidence on the Polygraph. Division of Behavioral and Social Sciences and Education. Washington, D.C.: The National Academies Press.

Barry, Anita M. (2005). *Report of Pneumonic Tularemia in Three Boston University Researchers.* Boston, Mass., Boston Public Health Commission.

"Biological Defense Safety Program and Technical Safety Requirements" *Federal Register.* Vol. 71(236), 32 CFR parts 626 and 627, December 8 2006.

U.S. Department of Health and Human Services Centers for Disease Control and Prevention and National Institutes of Health (2007). *Biosafety in Microbiological and Biomedical Laboratories* (BMBL) 5th Edition. Washington, D.C.: U.S. Government Printing Office.

Department of Health and Human Services, Centers for Disease Control and Prevention (June 30, 2007). "Subject: Suspension of Select Agent Work: Texas A&M University," Memorandum.

"Biosafety Lab Passes Disaster Test" *Nature* Vol 455; October 23, 2008.

Government Accountability Office (2008). *Biosafety Laboratories: Perimeter Security Assessment of the Nation's Five BSL-4 Laboratories.* GAO-08-1092. Washington, D.C.: US Government Printing Office.

Gronvall, Gigi Kwik and Nidhi Bouri. 2008. "Biosafety Laboratories." *Biosecurity and Bioterrorism: Biodefense Strategy, Practice, and Science* Vol. 6(4):300.

Regulations

Army Regulation 190-51 (Security of Unclassified Army Property)

Army Regulation 190-13 (The Army Physical Security Program)

Biosafety in Microbiological and Biomedical Laboratories (BMBL), 4th ed. (CDC)

42 CFR 72.6 effective 15 APR 1997, Regulated Transfer and Receipt of Select Agents by CDC

42 CFR 73 (Select Agent Rules, FEB 2003 is interim rule, MAR 2005 final rule; includes theft, loss, and release reporting requirement)

Biosafety in Microbiological and Biomedical Laboratories, 5th ed. (CDC)

DoD Directive 5210.88 (Safeguarding Biological Select Agents and Toxins)

DoD Instruction 5210.89 (Minimum Security Safeguards for Biological Select Agent and Toxins)

Army Interim Guidance Messages:

- #1: Implementing the Army Biological Surety Program, 21 DEC 2001

- #2: Establishing the Army Biological Surety PRP, 04 FEB 2002

- #3: Applicability of the Army Biological Surety Program to Contractor Operations, 07 FEB 2002

- #4: Implementing DoD Interim Biological Agent Security Policy, 29 JUL 2003

Army Regulation 50-X (28 DEC 2004) (Army Biological Surety Program)

Army Regulation 50-1 (effective date 28 OCT 2008) (Army Biological Surety Program)

Army Regulation 190-17 (Biological Select Agent and Toxin Security Program; includes theft and loss reporting requirement)

Army Regulation 190-11 (Physical Security of Arms, Ammunition, and Explosives)

Army Regulation 190-56 (The Army Civilian Police and Security Guard Program)

32 CFR parts 626 and 627, Biological Defense Safety Program and Technical Safety Requirements

Glossary

ACS	access control system
AFI	Air Force Instruction
AFRIMS	Armed Forces Research Institute of the Medical Sciences
ANCAI	Access NACI
APHIS	Animal and Plant Health Inspection Service
AR	Army Regulation
AT&L	Acquisition, Technology, and Logistics
BBRC	Battelle Biomedical Research Center
BMBL	Bio-Safety in Microbiological and Biomedical Labs
BPRP	Biological Personnel Reliability Program
BSAT	biological select agents and toxins
BSL – 1/2/3/4	Biological Safety Level–One/Two/Three/Four
BU	Boston University
CBR	Chemical, Biological, and Radiological
CCTV	closed circuit television
CDC	Centers for Disease Control and Prevention
CFR	Code of Federal Regulations
CMA	Certifying Medical Authority
CO	Certifying Official
CONUS	continental United States
DAIG	Department of the Army Inspector General
DARPA	Defense Advanced Research Projects Agency
DCII	Defense Clearance and Investigations Index
DHS	Department of Homeland Security
DNA	Deoxyribonucleic acid
DoD	Department of Defense
DODD	Department of Defense Directive
DODI	Department of Defense Instruction
DOE	Department of Energy
DOJ	Department of Justice
DTRA	Defense Threat Reduction Agency
DSB	Defense Science Board
ECBC	Edgewood Chemical Biological Center
EQPT	equipment
FBI	Federal Bureau of Investigation

GAO	Government Accountability Office
HEPA	High Efficiency Particulate Air
HHS	Department of Health and Human Services
HPW	Human Performance Wing
HQDA	Headquarters of Department of Army
IT	information technology
JPAS	Joint Personnel Adjudication System
MRI	Midwest Research Institute
NAC	National Agency Check
NACI	NAC and Inquiries
NACIC	NACI and Credit
NACLC	NAC with Local Agency Check and Credit
NBACC	National Biodefense Analysis and Countermeasure Center
NAMRU-3	Naval Medical Research Unit No. 3
NCPRP	Nuclear Chemical Personnel Reliability Program
NEIDL	National Emerging Infectious Diseases Laboratories
NIAID	National Institute of Allergy and Infectious Diseases
NIH	National Institutes of Health
NET OPS	Network Operations
NIPRNET	Non-Classified Internet Protocol Router Network
NMRC	Naval Medical Research Center
NMRCD	Naval Medical Research Center Detachment
NPRP	Nuclear Personnel Reliability Program
NSA	National Security Agency
NSWCDD	Naval Surface Warfare Center – Dahlgren Division
OCONUS	outside the Continental United States
OPM	Office of Personnel Management
OPNAVINST	Chief of Naval Operations instruction
PL	Public Law
PRP	Personnel Reliability Program
PSI	Personnel Security Investigation
RNA	Ribonucleic Acid
RDT&E	Research, Development, Test & Evaluation
RF	Radio Frequency
RMC	Rocky Mountain Laboratories
RO	Responsible Official
SCADA	Supervisory Control and Data Acquisition
SOP	Standard Operating Procedure
SRA	Security Risk Assessment

SSBI	Single Scope Background Investigation
SSBI-PR	Single Scope Background Investigation-Periodic Reinvestigation
SSI	Security/Sustainability Investigation
USAMC	United States Army Medical Component
USAMRICD	United States Army Medical Research Institute of Chemical Defense
USDA	United States Department of Agriculture
UTMB	University of Texas—Medical Branch
UPS	United Postal Service
USAMRIID	U.S. Army Medical Research Institute for Infectious Diseases
USD	Under Secretary of Defense
USDA	U.S. Department of Agriculture
VIC	Viral Immunology Center
WRAIR	Walter Reed Army Institute of Research
WDTC	West Desert Test Center